RADICAL ABUNDANCE

MORE THAN ALL WE CAN ASK OR IMAGINE

Compiled and Introduced by Teresa Janzen

ISBN: 979-8-9857499-3-9 (PRINT)

ISBN: 979-8-9857499-4-6 (EBOOK)

Published by Abundance Books
417 Forest St. #445
Kalamazoo, MI 49001

abundance-books.com

Table of Contents

God's Faithfulness Through the Generations

Introduction

by Teresa Janzen

At a neighborhood coffee hour at a local church, the weathered man sitting next to me remarked, "I've attended Alcoholics Anonymous meetings at this church for years, but I'd never be welcomed on a Sunday morning." Before I could object, he continued, "I'd probably let a swear word slip, and then I'd be shown the door."

Is it possible that the people who need the church most are excluded because of social and cultural behavior? Isn't the church meant to lead people to repentance and salvation so that they can experience a vibrant and transformed life? Have you ever experienced disunity or been unfairly excluded in some way?

Ephesians was written primarily to new Gentile believers in and around Ephesus. It is a *circular* letter designed to be read aloud and shared among many congregations. Letters like this were also called *pastoral* letters because they were meant to guide the church in resolving a particular problem.

At first glance, Ephesians seems to be a bit more general, talking about theological issues like salvation through faith alone, and the blessing found in Christ's resurrection. But perhaps the underlying problem being addressed in the letter was so widespread that it seemed almost normal.

An *us* vs. them atmosphere had infiltrated the Church, causing disunity. The idea of Salvation by faith was radical to Jewish believers who treasured tradition. Though Jewish leaders knew the Torah to affirm a faith-based relationship with God, "Abram believed the LORD, and he credited it to him as righteousness," (Genesis 15:6 NIV), they clung to tradition and wanted to impose it on new converts as well. After all, it was the law that had taught God's chosen people how to be followers of the Most High.

What must it have been like to be a Gentile believer? Like a new kid on the first day of school, they may have been tempted to shrink into the shadows searching for cues for right behavior from the in-crowd. But could the in-crowd be trusted to exemplify good behavior?

Jesus broke all the rules and included people previously excluded from the in-crowd. Today, we have the benefit of both the foundational truth of the Old Testament and the illuminating revelation that Jesus provided through his teaching. As a result, we can see God's love for all people is recorded from Genesis to Revelation.

Therefore, the book of Ephesians was written to illustrate what it is to be unified in Christ. The first half of the letter outlines the foundation of faith in the miraculous work of Christ's substitutionary death and victorious resurrection. Since it is Christ's work that has brought salvation to all who believe, there is no place for one group of Christians to feel more than, or less than, another. This served as an encouragement to Gentile believers as well as instructional teaching to their Jewish counterparts.

The second half of the letter focuses on applying the Christian faith to life in the church, family, and community. Where some people have chosen to single out select verses as doctrinal statements, I prefer to view the text as a continuation on the theme of unity with specific examples that address societal issues relevant to the early church.

At the center of the letter, the author makes a proclamation that bridges the theology of faith with the practical application of what faith should look like in daily life.

> *Now to him who is able to do immeasurably more than all we ask or imagine, according to his power that is at work within us, to him be glory in the church and in Christ Jesus throughout all generations, for ever and ever! Amen.*
>
> Ephesians 3:20-21 (NIV)

This passage serves as a conclusion to the first half of the letter and an introduction to the latter. This book is a collection of devotionals organized around four themes inspired by this key passage:

- God's answers for the unimaginable
- God's power over the impossible
- God's glory through his church
- God's faithfulness in the family

God's answers for the unimaginable features prayers that were lifted before God amid challenging circumstances. Sometimes the answers were miraculous and other times they were unexpected and seemingly delayed. In each story, we see that God *is able to do immeasurably more than all we ask or imagine.* If you need an answer from God today, know that he is able. We may not always understand his ways, but we can trust that his plan is beyond our imagination. We will see it when the time is right.

God's power over the impossible demonstrates God's sovereignty, which surpasses every other power. It's a transformative *power at work within us*. The same power that raised Christ from the dead is the power at work in our lives today (Ephesians 1:19-20). Regardless of your circumstances, God's power is at work within you and within your life.

God's glory through his church is inspired by times when the body of Christ fulfills its mandate. Whether making disciples (Matthew 28:19-20), visiting widows and orphans (James 1:27), caring for the vulnerable (Matthew 25:34-36), or speaking against injustice (Micah 6:8), God calls the church to transform culture and engage society in a way that glorifies God *in the church and in Christ Jesus.*

God's faithfulness in the family recounts stories from the heart of our most vulnerable place—the family. God has a multigenerational approach to his redemptive plan. As he has been faithful to his people through all kinds of adversity, we can also see his hand at work *throughout all generations.*

It has been my pleasure to introduce each section with a devotional from this key passage followed by contributions from other authors. You won't find a strict alignment to the categories, as many of the stories could have been placed in more than one section. Each author has shared from his or her own experience and in his or her own style. It is my hope that the variety in this collection will bring a radical abundance of faith to your daily time of reflection.

God's Answers for the Unimaginable

How Could It Happen?

by Teresa Janzen

Now to him who is able to do far more abundantly than all that we ask or think, according to the power at work within us

Ephesians 3:20 (ESV)

Glued to the phone, I waited for my mother to call with word about my brother Jerry. I thought it was just another surgery—one more in a long list of surgeries over the years since his motorcycle accident. Unlike past procedures, this was an elective straightening of the spine so Jerry might learn to walk again. But this time, something went wrong.

I was eleven years old when Jerry had his accident, which left him wheelchair-bound. On several occasions, Mom had to make the decision of whether to allow the doctors to turn off life support. Every time she refused, and every time Jerry pulled through.

When the phone finally rang, Mom's voice was calm but quiet. "It's over. Jerry died," she said.

My mind spun out of control. How could that be possible? Everything was finally going well. He was going to learn to walk. The next clear memory I have is walking past the blue, fabric-covered box containing my brother's earthly remains to deliver his eulogy.

The idea that Jerry might die never crossed my mind—not at the time of his accident fourteen years earlier, nor after the first phone call when mom reported his distress during surgery. He had been through so much worse and had always been fine. This surgery wasn't even required; it was just to improve his balance during physical therapy. I was certain God had big plans for my brother. That's why he had survived the accident years before and all the events that followed. I was waiting for the miracle I knew would happen someday.

Right about now, you might be wondering if you are reading the right devotional book. Aren't we supposed to be talking about God's power to answer prayer in radically abundant ways beyond our imagination? But that's the problem. Our ideas are always about our plans and our hopes. God's plans go way beyond anything we can imagine.

Sometimes God's answers don't look like we expect. If he is "able to do far more abundantly than all that we ask or think," why doesn't he? The truth is our scope of the situation is limited, while God's is limitless. We have to trust God, even when we don't understand.

I don't know why my brother had a motorcycle accident when he was just sixteen years old, and I don't know why he died during an elective procedure fourteen years later. But I can glimpse parts of God's plan. Hundreds of people were touched by my brother's wit and intellect, once they got past his shocking physical appearance. Part of who I am is a result of being brought up in a family undergoing extreme challenges. Yet the full scope of God's plan for my brother's short life remains a mystery.

God's answers are good. Not because they fulfill our desires, but because he is good and sees the story from beginning to end. Spending time in God's Word helps me focus on his big plan rather than comparing my prayer outcome with that of others.

Have you ever prayed for something and been confused—even devastated—by the outcome? How did you find purpose and peace when things didn't go the way you expected?

Mighty God, nothing is impossible for you, yet I confess that I sometimes don't understand your ways. I know you can see beyond my circumstances, and you know the larger plan for me and this world. Help me to pray with confidence and trust the outcome to you. Amen.

"

You Will Reap

by Penny Cooke

For in due season we shall reap if we do not lose heart

Galatians 6:9 (NKJV)

Thoughtful, sensitive, humorous, creative and talented is how I described my son when he was young. But his character had changed. His music changed. His friends changed. The way he dressed changed. He became disinterested in the things he used to enjoy, like drawing and playing the guitar.

One day while searching his room for a clue to what was going on, I found a hole in the wallboard in his closet. I inserted my hand to see what I might find, and I cut my finger on a razor blade. My heart bled heavier than my finger.

One particular Thanksgiving, my parents took us out for dinner. Our son sat across the table falling asleep, which was becoming a regular event. He would sneak out his window at night. My husband had to bolt the window shut.

There were arrests, short drug programs, and periods when we didn't know where he was. We agonized what to do and felt powerless as we watched him drowning in the quicksand of drugs. Many times parents' efforts to help their prodigal only enables them further.

I wearied of praying the same thing over and over. Were my prayers hitting the ceiling? Would God ever answer? I knew so many kids who didn't make it. Would he be one of them? Fear and discouragement would have made me lose heart if it wasn't for God's Word and prayer. I found comfort in the Psalms and turned many into prayers for him.

But still, the long, painful road seemed unending.

The situation intensified further when he stole from us. We knew this was not who he is and that his actions were led by the need for another fix, but it was time for tough love. My husband gave him an ultimatum: go to a year-long, faith-based rehabilitation program, or he would file charges against him.

He chose to run. While he ran from that warrant for almost two years, I continued to pray Scripture over him, and I watered those prayers with my tears. Then one day, after thirteen years of addiction and exhausting all his possibilities with family and friends, he cried out, "God, if you're real, I need help."

A few days later, he was arrested and brought back to our county jail. The short story of his long journey is that he entered a year-long, faith-based rehabilitation program. While there, he felt led to go to Bible college. He is now a pastor, with a wonderful, godly wife and two adorable children.

God did above and beyond anything I ever prayed. I longed for my son to be free of drugs, but God gave him, and me, far more than anything I could imagine.

Arm yourself with the Sword of the Spirit when you face a spiritual battle. What Scripture can you turn into a prayer that encourages and strengthens when you are losing heart?

Lord, when it feels like you're not listening, help me trust that you are working. You know what is best. You will answer in your better way and time. Help me stay in your Word and keep praying so I won't lose heart. Thank you that your plan is better than anything I could ask for. I will reap the prayers I've watered with tears.

In Jesus' mighty name, amen.

"

....
....
....
....
....
....
....
....
....
....
....
....
....
....

Do You Trust Me?

by Sarah Griffiths Hu

He will tend his flock like a shepherd; he will gather the lambs in his arms; he will carry them in his bosom, and gently lead those that are with young.

Isaiah 40:11 (ESV)

The riverside trail wasn't where I wanted to be. I hated walking alone, but I wasn't ready to go home. Too many emotions awaited me there, too many questions. I needed time with God, time by myself.

Gravel crunched under my feet as I zipped my jacket and turned up the collar. The trees weren't as bare today; little spots of green sprouted from the branches. The world was springing to life, but my world felt like it was crumbling.

My son was battling addiction, my daughter was recovering from another major surgery, and my husband had lost two clients. I felt helpless and confused.

"God, why? I think I'm losing my son; we have no money and my daughter is in too much pain. I'm not sure I can take one more thing. Please God, I don't know what to do."

His still, small voice penetrated my heart.

Do you trust me?

"Yes, God."

Do you know I love you?

"Yes, God."

Do you believe I love your family more than you do?

"Yes, God."

Do you trust me to take care of your family?

I stuffed my hands in my pockets and slowed my steps.

"Yes God, but—"

Dear one, do you trust me?

I sighed. "Yes, God, I trust you to care for my family."

Friend, I'd like to tell you that I went home and everything was perfect, but that's not always how God works. Yes, he does work miracles, but looking back, I feel he was leading me to learn to trust him with those most precious to me—my family.

God did save my son from addiction, but it took years. Every time I found myself overcome with worry, God would remind me to let go and trust my son to him. Miraculously, my daughter healed six weeks ahead of schedule, and doctors were amazed. And God brought more clients my husband's way.

Trusting God with our loved ones may feel more challenging than trusting him with our own lives. We often worry and fret about their safety. Still, God faithfully reminds us that we don't have to worry because he is in control. In the darkest valley or on the highest mountain peak, God sits with us. Sometimes he carries us, but he always gently guides us.

What is one thing you can trust God with today?

God, I give my loved ones to you and trust you to care for them. When worry begins to creep back in, remind me you are in control and love them far more than I do. Thank you for your love, your faithfulness, and your gentle guidance. Amen.

“

....
....
....
....
....
....
....
....
....
....
....
....
....
....

The Journey Home

by Leann Seale

He made from one blood all nations who live on the earth. He set the times and places where they should live.

Acts 17:26 (NLV)

Our family earnestly prayed that God would make a way for us to move to a house in Glendora, CA, a city nestled at the base of the foothills where my husband and I grew up. Our family, friends, church, and schools were there, and we longed for a home where our four boys could bring their friends and we could use for ministry. Housing prices were sky high, but that didn't stop our search.

One of our sons and I found the perfect house for our family within walking distance of two of our schools, and the floor plan was ideal for large gatherings. This new house was one of ten being built on our church's old property. However, my hopes were crushed when my husband took one look at the listing price and declared it way out of our price range.

Over the next couple of years, we continued to pray. We had been commuting to school and church events, but in the fall one of our boys would be attending high school, another attending middle school, and two attending elementary school. We stepped up our nightly prayers around the dinner table, asking God to help us find a home close to our schools before fall.

We looked at many houses, placed offers, and felt disappointment as hopes turned into tears. At a Christian family camp we attended during summer, we were reminded of Acts 17:26, and continued to trust that God had a place for us in his perfect timing.

Our best friends were also looking to buy a house that summer and had bought one of the ten houses on the old church property. They informed us that the builder-owner was working on deals to get families in and had cut the price since these houses had been sitting for nearly two years after the housing market crash.

Sure enough, God made a way when there was no way. We ended up buying the house I had fallen in love with two years prior, and we were just four houses down from our friends. By the grace of God and in his perfect timing, we moved in two days before school started, and the boys walked to school!

There was no doubt this house was a gift from God. We promised to use it for his glory, and for the past twelve years, we have hosted many family and friends, as well as prayer, disciple group, couples ministry, youth group and Young Life meetings.

The beautiful part of God's faithfulness is that I gave my heart to Jesus back in seventh grade on this same church property, my first church home. Now our family lives here. God loves to knock our socks off with his gracious goodness and provision. Our family learned to pray and trust God, who places us where we live for a time and purpose, that we may be used by him for his glory.

Is there a circumstance in your life that is weighing on you? Consider giving it to God in prayer, then trust and wait on his perfect timing.

Dear Heavenly Father, You hear my prayers and know the desires of my heart. You give good gifts to your children, in your perfect timing, and I am grateful to be called yours. You care about the details of my life, and I am known and loved by you. Praise you and thank you for who you are, and who you call me to be. In Jesus' name, amen.

“

....
....
....
....
....
....
....
....
....
....
....
....
....
....

Celestial Piano Lessons

by Roberta Sarver

Ask, and it shall be given you; seek, and ye shall find; knock, and it shall be opened unto you.

Matthew 7:7 (KJV)

Our church pianist was every song leader's dream. Ron could play any song in any key, with or without written music. His complex chords and creative progressions set a worshipful tone for congregational singing. If someone suddenly broke into song, this virtuoso's fingers instantly picked up the tune and provided heart-warming accompaniment.

Soloists appreciated Ron's professional accompaniment. His unique method served to enhance their sometimes-amateur voices and made them appear several notches above their skill level.

As an accompanist on the church organ, I appreciated the privilege of lending my limited skill to Ron's stellar technique. Perhaps if I kept the volume down, people scarcely would notice.

To our chagrin, this musical prodigy moved to another state, leaving a huge void in the worship services. What to do? We had others who could play the piano, but none equaled the one we lost.

Sometimes the pastor's wife can be drafted to fill vacancies in places where she doesn't feel comfortable. This was one of those places. By virtue of my position, the board elected me to take Ron's place.

It was a humbling experience. A year of secular college piano lessons hadn't prepared me to arrange chords and progressions that lent dignity to majestic hymns and exuberance to lilting gospel tunes. No one complained, but I felt like a child playing "Chopsticks" for a crowd at Carnegie Hall.

This went on for some time. One day, sitting at the ebony grand piano in the empty sanctuary, I prayed a simple prayer. "Lord, the worship service isn't the same without Ron's beautiful music. Could you teach me to play better than I know how so the service will be a blessing?"

God answered that prayer progressively. From that point on, when I played for worship services, I noticed a gradual change. If I tried to play simple chords I knew, my fingers hit more complex ones which I had previously struggled to locate. Then I applied those to other songs. Over a span of months, God changed my piano technique in answer to that simple prayer. We received a blessing as beautiful, anointed music filled the church once more.

Our youth leader approached me after several weeks and said, "I notice your piano playing is different than it used to be." Yes, it was, thanks to God who answered more abundantly than I could ask or think.

A simple prayer, for God's glory, yielded results far beyond my imagination.

What challenging situation motivates you to see God's glory manifested?

Dear Heavenly Father, you have answered prayer through the ages in so many creative ways. Please help me ask, seek, and knock with your glory as my goal. In Christ's name, amen.

"

....
....
....
....
....
....
....
....
....
....
....
....
....
....

Beyond My Dreams

by Sandra Hastings

If ye then, being evil, know how to give good gifts unto your children, how much more shall your Father which is in heaven give good things to them that ask him?

Matthew 7:11 (KJV)

We had to move, but where? Our church people in Germany had been meeting in our home. Now they'd bought a building, and this meant we would also need a new place to live. In the past, we had lived in old apartments or houses with small rooms and windows, radiator heating, no yard, and unfinished kitchens.

Since only the Lord knew what our health and finances would be in the future and who he wanted us to have for neighbors, I decided to leave the choice entirely up to him. My only request was that he would make it very clear that it was the place he wanted us to have. In my heart, I was preparing myself to do with less than we had before.

One day we received a call about a house coming available. We got the address, made an appointment to see it, and then checked out the location. I was overwhelmed. It was a new, modern house with lots of big windows and only three blocks from the new church building. Immediately, I told my husband it was just too good for us and could not imagine living there.

The scheduled day to see the house arrived, and I could hardly control my excitement as we walked through it. It had a beautiful kitchen, heated white tile floors, plenty of space, a marble staircase, and a corner bathtub, which my husband had always wanted. To top it off, it was in our price range. We told the owners we would let them know our answer the next day. However, when we called to accept the house, they said they had put an ad in the area newspaper and wanted to wait to see who responded. They promised to let us know by the following Monday.

However, Wednesday came, and still no phone call. I was convinced the owners had decided not to give the house to us. I told the Lord it was okay. I didn't need all the niceties anyway, and again I searched the ads. I even made an appointment to see an apartment the following Friday.

When I came home from shopping on Thursday, my husband informed me that the owners of the beautiful house had called. He looked quite serious and, assuming I knew what he was going to say, I said, "It's okay honey. I don't need it."

I could hardly believe my ears when my husband informed me that the owners had decided to give the house to us and wanted to sign the contract that evening. I was shocked and excited, but most of all, overwhelmed by God's goodness.

That evening, when we arrived at the landlord's home, they explained they had trouble deciding between three different families. They believed picking us was their choice, but I knew it was the Lord's special gift to us.

In what area of your life do you need to yield your desires and will to Jesus Christ, allowing him to have absolute control?

Dear Lord, forgive me when I make decisions without seeking your will. Please help me to trust you and willingly relinquish my desires for what you have planned for me. Thank you, Father, for your love and faithfulness, for your patience and mercy. In Jesus' name, amen.

“

....
....
....
....
....
....
....
....
....
....
....
....
....
....

Enough For Any Circumstance

by Heather MacAskill

Therefore we do not lose heart. Though outwardly we are wasting away, yet inwardly we are being renewed day by day.

2 Corinthians 4:16 (NIV)

It had been a long year. My fight against cancer was physically and emotionally draining. Jesus had stayed close, giving strength and comfort. I was completely assured of his presence. Slowly, pieces of my life were returning. Physical strength was improving and the treatments were almost done. I felt on the verge of normal.

Then the news came that buckled my knees. The cancer was back. Tests indicated cancer had returned to my brain, and also a couple of places in my torso. Just when I thought the battle was ending, cancer suddenly regrouped and came charging back.

Through the previous year, I had been given many opportunities to share my testimony. Another one was scheduled for that month. With the news of the cancer being back, I didn't feel like I could do it. I told God I wasn't able to do it. No one would blame me for backing out. I had a good reason. But God wouldn't let me off the hook. I had to use the opportunity he had given me. So I prepared, prayed really hard, and made the podcast recording.

It was really God who spoke that night. As I shared, I felt energy and peace. I knew God was giving me strength. He was enough, even in uncertainty. While outwardly everything looked like it was falling apart, inwardly I was being renewed. I had the confidence that Jesus was in control. It's so easy to lose heart. Circumstances can barge in and take over, filling our minds with fear and anxiety. That's when we need to check where our focus is. When our minds and hearts are focused on Jesus, not a day goes by without his amazing grace pouring into us and sustaining us.

I was totally unprepared for the response to that podcast. Because it was shared over social media, suddenly I had people I didn't know praying for me. I received such encouraging messages. Here I was, in the middle of a battle, facing uncertainty, and yet God was asking me to do something. I didn't want to do it, didn't think I could do it, but he was enough for me. He gave me strength, words, and peace. Then he turned around and used it to not only glorify himself, but also to give me increased prayer support. He gave me what I needed, exactly when I needed it.

Six weeks later, we met with the oncologist to get results of more tests. As she started to share the results of the tests, she fumbled a bit, seemingly searching for words. Then she paused and looked up at us. "I was wrong. The cancer is not back. That area in the brain that was growing doesn't have any blood flowing to it. The other spots we saw are gone. As of right now, we consider you cancer free." God had worked a miraculous healing!

What circumstances are pulling your eyes away from what Jesus is offering you?

Jesus, thank you that you know all the intimate details of every circumstance we are facing. We surrender those details into your loving hands, and ask that you bring our focus back onto you. Sustain us with your peace and strength. When it feels like things are falling apart, Lord remind us of the grace that you stand ready to pour into our lives.

❝

....
....
....
....
....
....
....
....
....
....
....
....
....
....

Sometimes Less is More

by Mary Harker

The thief's purpose is to steal and kill and destroy. My purpose is to give them a rich and satisfying life.

John 10:10 (NLT)

I was one of those little girls who grew up dreaming of being a mommy one day. I played house with my dolls for hours on end. My younger sister is ten years younger than me and was my live baby doll (to my mother's dismay). I imagined having a large family someday. I came from a family of four, which seemed like the perfect number.

Then one day, at the beginning of my second year of nursing school, I received a phone call. The housemother of our dorm came on the intercom in my room, "Mary, you have a call on line 2" (yes, I'm ancient, and this was before cell phones).

"Thanks, Mrs. Moe," I replied, "I got it." And I ran down the hall to the phone booth. (I told you I was ancient.) That call changed my life forever. My doctor gave me the news that I would never be able to conceive children. I was devastated, and my dreams were shattered.

However, through the years, I did not give up the hope of a

family. Instead, I prayed God would somehow intervene and give me a miraculous pregnancy. I bought a stuffed bunny I planned to give my future child (this was after I heard the story of a woman who kept a pair of men's jeans at the end of her bed and prayed for a husband to fill them). I claimed all of the promises that God would give me all that I asked for.

During this time, I learned a lesson I will never forget. God is not a celestial Santa Claus who brings all of our wishes into reality. He is a loving, heavenly Father who knows what is best for us. In the above verse, some versions say that he (Jesus) came so we might have an abundant life. The Greek word for abundant here is perissos. It can mean superior, extraordinary, surpassing, uncommon. I interpreted this verse to mean God will bless us with more than we ask or think. And that is true. He can give us more than we expect in huge numbers or miracles. But it's not always the case. Just like the quality of a meal at an exquisite restaurant can be more satisfying than a heaping buffet, sometimes less is more.

My husband and I adopted a beautiful son from Russia when I was in my early forties. I never carried a child in my womb, nor did we adopt more than one child. But God gave us a single gift that is superior and surpassed anything I could have prayed for. Our son has brought richness and satisfaction to our lives. And I have learned to seek the giver and not just the gifts.

So dear one, maybe you feel your life is less than abundant. I encourage you to look to the giver of all good gifts and experience his satisfaction. Sometimes less is more.

When you experience loss or disappointment, how can you taste the rich and satisfying life Jesus wants to give you?

Heavenly Father, thank you for all the blessings you have given me. When the enemy tries to steal, lie, and destroy, help me to encounter your rich and satisfying life. I want to seek you alone and not just your gifts.

“

....
....
....
....
....
....
....
....
....
....
....
....
....
....

Consider the Lilies

by Nancy Lee Jenkins

Consider the lilies how they grow: they toil not, they spin not; and yet I say unto you, that Solomon in all his glory was not arrayed like one of these.

Luke 12:27 (KJV)

While driving to work a frightening thought came to me, "If I were to drive off a cliff, no one would miss me." I was twenty-nine, married with children, going through a third try at marriage counseling. I felt empty inside. Hot tears began to flow, streaming down my cheeks, so fast I couldn't see to drive. Pulling over to the side of the road, I covered my face, letting the tears spill.

Gathering my emotions, memories of my youth came flooding back, days when God and church were important. Realizing how far I had drifted, I cried out, "God, help! I need you!" Please forgive me for the poor choices I've made. Repenting, I pleaded with God to take me back into His care. "I want to turn my life over to you. If you can do anything with the mess I've made, I'm all yours! Change me!"

Knowing I was forgiven, I pulled back onto the highway with peace and a new direction in life. I had returned to the God of my childhood.

That night at our last counseling session a voice of authority from inside me arose. "I'm going to start going to church, and I'm taking the kids with me." I was as surprised as my husband Joe, but he replied, "I don't care. Go to church if you want."

I was attending church for about three months when I wanted a dress to wear like the ladies I saw every Sunday. I mentioned it to the girls at work. One said, "I have one that will fit you." It was a dark brown knit. I wore that dress every Sunday for many months, till Joe said one day, "If you want to go to church Sunday you will have to find a different dress to wear. I will not let you leave wearing that brown dress again." And so I prayed, "Lord, Help! Sunday is only a few days away; I have no money to shop!"

At work that night a customer told me of her sister, who had bought a new wardrobe. Could I make use of some good used clothes, and would I be willing to get them? "Oh, Yes!" I replied. I had to make two trips to carry the seven large boxes filled with beautiful, stylish clothes.

When Joe came home that night our house looked like a department store, with clothes draped in every room. I was thanking and praising the Lord while selecting my favorites.

It was a quiet night. While reading my Bible, I learned about God's lilies growing in a field that were dressed better than King Solomon. I have received many compliments concerning my Sunday outfits since that day. I always feel special, as one of God's lilies because I have learned that God's supply is of the best quality and can come in great abundance.

When have you been blessed beyond your expectation?

Thank you Lord, for letting me be your child and meeting all my needs in special ways. You always give me more than I deserve. I am grateful for your love and care. Your blessings keep me and my home well dressed, as I share your salvation as a king's kid.

“

....
....
....
....
....
....
....
....
....
....
....
....
....
....

Heart for the Nations

by Melissa Heiland

Or which one of you, if his son asks him for bread, will give him a stone? Or if he asks for a fish, will give him a serpent? If you then, who are evil, know how to give good gifts to your children, how much more will your Father who is in heaven give good things to those who ask him!

Matthew 7:9-11 (ESV)

When I was a young mother, the Lord called me to be a missionary. It was something that came out of the blue, or so it seemed to my young mind. As I was growing up in the church, I was never interested in missions. Missionaries' lives seemed dull to me and I didn't like their clothes. It's embarrassing to share this now, but it is the truth. So, when the Lord inexplicably placed a burden for missions on my heart, I was taken completely by surprise, but I wanted to obey. My husband was not at all interested and so I prayed and waited. I knew the Lord would not call me without my husband, so I waited for him to change either Ken's heart or mine.

After a year of changes and profound loss, the Lord called my husband to missions and we began the exciting process of becoming missionaries. We sold all our belongings, attended missionary school, and moved our young family of five overseas for what I thought would be the rest of our lives.

After one short year on the mission field, the Lord called us back to the United States. We were hurt and bewildered. We could not imagine why the Lord would give us a passion for missions and then call us back to the United States. We returned to the US in obedience to God, but we had no understanding of what God had planned for us. I felt lost and alone. I begged him to allow me to serve as a missionary.

The Lord began, almost immediately, to reveal his plan. He allowed us to begin taking teams overseas to serve on short-term mission trips. We were able to share our love for the nations with many who grew to love missions as well. Over time, he showed me that his plan for me was to begin international pregnancy centers. We began a missions organization that plants pregnancy ministries worldwide. We have had the incredible privilege of serving in over 20 nations and on 5 continents. I thought we would serve in only one nation, but God has given us the world. I learned that when God takes something from you, it is because he wants to give you something better. His plans are greater than ours. We can trust him, even when we do not understand.

Throughout my life, I have seen the goodness of the Lord. I have seen his love and care for me and my family through times of tragedy and loss, as well as in times of blessing. God has been faithful to answer every prayer in ways that are so much greater than I could ever imagine. Never be afraid to ask the Lord to meet your deepest needs. He knows your needs and longs to give you the desires of your heart. Trust that he will use even the darkest of times, to draw you close to him and use you for his glory.

In what area of your life do you long to see God move?

Dear Father, I thank you that you are a good God. You love your children and shower us with good gifts. You are faithful and your timing is perfect. Help me trust you even when I do not understand. Thank you for your love and kindness. In Jesus' name, amen.

“

....
....
....
....
....
....
....
....
....
....
....
....
....
....

God's Fingerprints

by Nancy Kay Grace

It is the Lord who goes before you. He will be with you; he will not leave you or forsake you. Do not fear or be dismayed.

Deuteronomy 31:8 (ESV)

God coordinated our meeting a foreign exchange student in a rural Kansas community that led my husband and I to go serve a church in a former communist country.

This opportunity pushed me way out of my comfort zone. My pastor-husband Rick would teach the church leaders. Uncertain of my role in this ministry, I packed translated Bible studies for women as well as children's ministry materials.

We then traveled by ourselves to that faraway country. On the long flight, I prayed and journaled every concern in my heart. Page after page was filled with requests for safe connections, health, and the desire to be used by God.

When we landed, we found our first answered prayer. Those who had promised to meet us, including the foreign-exchange student who had launched us on this journey, were there at the airport. Relief washed over me. However, another request was added to my prayer journal—one of my bags did not arrive.

Experiencing a different country is challenging and eye opening. There's joy in partnering with God, but also weariness from unfamiliarity with the culture. Midway through our time there, I felt worn down from translation issues and the unending foreign sounds of the language. I yearned for familiarity.

Each morning, we headed down the dim hotel stairwell for the same breakfast. However, one particular day stands out from the rest.

On the stairs, we crossed paths with two women whom we had met the previous night at a meeting with other Americans. They had recently arrived. One cheerful woman asked if they could pray for us. In our tiredness, we agreed. I'll never forget their prayer in that stairwell.

"Lord, let them be helplessly dependent on You."

The prayer brought a new infusion of faith, strengthening me to finish strong. God sent these women to pray and encourage us at just the right time.

In the remainder of our time there, The Lord enabled me to share the resurrection story with children who had never heard it. The translated Bible study materials were given to one of the women to share with others, and we left supplies for use in their children's ministry. Our hearts were full from seeing God at work in a different culture and in us.

The long flight home provided ample time to reflect on the experience. I re-read my prayer journal, writing "AP" (answered prayer) by every request. God used everything in my suitcases, even the late-arriving bag.

The Lord went before me, and I met Him beyond my

comfort zone—in the trust zone. His fingerprints were in the answered prayers along the way. The experience stretched my faith and strengthened my trust in the Lord. God broke through language and cultural barriers. His love was with us in our connections with believers on the other side of the world, and also strength in our weariness. The Lord replaced the apprehension of leaving my comfort zone with confidence in Him through the abundance of answered prayers.

How have you seen God's fingerprints in everyday life and when you least expect it?

Lord, thank you for your promise to never leave me, no matter where I am, whether in my comfort zone or beyond it. Open my eyes every day to see your fingerprints in the world around me. Enable me to share your love, knowing that you are with me in every situation. In the name of Jesus, amen.

“

....
....
....
....
....
....
....
....
....
....
....
....
....
....

After the Storm

by Chrischa Marie Q. Rosalejos

But he said to me, "My grace is sufficient for you, for my power is made perfect in weakness."
Therefore I will boast all the more gladly about my weaknesses, so that Christ's power may rest on me.
2 Corinthians 12:9 (NIV)

It was 16 December, 2021 when Super Typhoon Rai, also known locally as Odette, hit the Philippines. The wind growled like a hungry lion and preyed on the tiny houses in our village. We were waiting for it to quiet down as we sat in complete darkness listening to the roar of the wind and waves. Would the roof and the feeble glass of the window panes protect us from this beast? Where would we go if our house was devoured?

The fallout was harder than the storm. The electricity was cut off and food and water were scarce. We lost internet access and, worst of all, there was no cell signal in our area. We had no way of communicating with anyone outside. I lost my online job because they had to fill the positions that were vacated during the typhoon. Then I lost my savings because we needed to use it to survive.

It was a total disaster.

We spent Christmas under the light of the moon and had a

candlelight dinner, which I think should have been romantic if it weren't for the circumstances. We spent New Year's Eve the same way. It was simple, but at least we were completely safe and able to celebrate the birth of our savior, Jesus Christ.

Then the questions came. How will I get a new job? How will I be able to help my family if I do not get one?

When communication was restored, I immediately set up things and tried to apply for jobs online. I failed a bunch of job interviews because I was new to it, but I did not give up. I kept on with the mindset that If I do not get in, it certainly is not for me and God wants me to keep going and seek other things. I kept on praying that wherever I landed, I wanted to be near him and know him more in the process.

I heard from a friend about Ripple VAs, but I was stubborn. I did not apply to it immediately. I was able to work and got accepted into a Digital Marketing Agency in Sydney, Australia as the Executive Assistant of the CEO. I thought everything was going well, but then one day I felt God whispering to me, saying, "This is not the way I want things for you to go".

That day was so incredible. I was able to muster up all my courage, mail my resignation letter, and submit my application for Ripple VAs. I learned so much, not just for my career but also about God. I sensed him there.

When I entered the agency, it just felt right. I got my first client—Teresa Janzen. My treasure sent from above. It was the easiest job interview of my life, and as a result, you are reading this testimony in this book! The rest of my clients flowed in afterward.

I realized that I could never outperform what God wants me to have.

All these changes and all the blessings I am receiving right now are not up to me, but by his will.

He may present us with challenges and obstacles in life, but there are times when this is merely his way to prepare us for something greater that is yet to come.

How have circumstances in your life changed the way you think about life and about how amazing his grace is?

Heavenly Father, you have blessed us in ways we could never imagine. We thank you for your glory and kindness. We ask for forgiveness for our sins. Aid us in declaring victory and increase for everyone. Help us to let love in and leave hate out. May we always speak about your greatness to other people.

In Jesus' holy name, amen.

“

....
....
....
....
....
....
....
....
....
....
....
....
....
....

God of the Meanwhiles

by Chaplain Lisa Northway, U.S. Army

When Abram was ninety-nine years old, the Lord appeared to him and said, "I am El-Shaddai, 'God Almighty.' Serve me faithfully and live a blameless life. I will make a covenant with you, by which I will guarantee to give you countless descendants."

Genesis 17:1-2 (NLT)

In our meanwhiles we need to allow God to stabilize us. Not only for the present, but also for the days ahead. Nothing looks as we think it should when we have worked, hoped, and prayed, but the expected outcome does not materialize in our preferred time frame. In addition, I tend to get impatient when I've worked hard and it appears my efforts are inadequate. It's in those moments I sense my spirit needs quieting.

Wherever the word meanwhile appears in the Bible, it usually reveals God is working on behalf of humanity. The life of Abraham and Sarah included a long meanwhile before they experienced the promise of God. Eventually they succumbed to taking matters into their own hands, causing much conflict in their household.

It can be similar for us today. During a challenging time

during a military course, I struggled academically and was at risk of failing, although the course leader confirmed I was doing all I could to graduate. After the oral exam, I was told to wait outside the classroom for my results. Meanwhile, in the hallway I prayed. God calmed my heart. Minutes later the door opened. To my relief I was called in to be congratulated for my passing grade. The next week on the written final, I missed passing the course by one point! I had to wait a month before an academic board voted to graduate me.

No one gets it right every time. We all need a Savior and Redeemer. God has our back no matter the outcome. Not only our back but also our face forward, each side of us, above and below. He knew we would face deep disappointment in ourselves, and each other. He knew we would be tempted to meddle in our own situations, allowing disappointment to meander our focus away from His original plan and intent for us.

My hope and prayer for each of us is that we would choose to trust God so we may know Christ as conqueror as well as the One Who is Present in our meanwhile. We can be empowered by the Holy Spirit to take right and better actions when we know to do so. May we step up to courageous acts of faith while in our meanwhile. Through Christ's conquering power, we can continue to step forward into the mission field God lovingly and strategically places us in.

What do you need to help you follow through with something the Holy Spirit may be prompting you to do? Are you in need of an accountability partner?

Ask God to bring to mind someone suitable for this season of the meanwhile in your life.

Dear Heavenly Father, please quiet my spirit to hear your voice and sense your loving comfort when what I experience causes me to doubt your presence and ability to impact my circumstances. Help me to know your stability in my meanwhile. Thank you for your faithfulness to me over my lifetime.

“

....
....
....
....
....
....
....
....
....
....
....
....
....
....

God's Power over the Impossible

A Drop in the Ocean

by Teresa Janzen

Now to him who is able to do far more abundantly than all that we ask or think, according to the power at work within us, to him be glory in the church and in Christ Jesus throughout all generations, forever and ever. Amen.

Ephesians 3:20-21 (ESV)

Like a toy boat bobbing in the water, waves lapped against the side of my plastic craft. I felt insignificant compared to the breadth of the lake surrounding me and the majesty of the mountains beyond. Awestruck by the grandeur of creation, I contemplated my purpose in the world. What did I have to offer that would make a difference any greater than a drop in the ocean?

God's power is manifest in the world around us every day. From northern mountain peaks veiled in dancing light to miniscule clumps of moss on the forest floor. I see God revealed in this amazing world, yet somehow my wonder evaporates when it comes to how I view myself.

Don't get me wrong; I think the human body is incredible. The way God made our bodies and minds to learn and grow and function is miraculous. But when I step back and look in the mirror, I don't get the same feeling of wonder as when I gaze at the stars in the sky.

The author of Ephesians talks about the power at work within us.

He uses the word power in several places in the letter when talking about the mystery of the Gospel being made available to all people. This power at work within us is God re-creating something extraordinary within the lives of those who have chosen to follow him.

When I reflect on what God has done and is still doing within me, I am overwhelmed with joy, gratitude, and humility. Today, I have healthier relationships with those around me and victory over the fear and obsessive behavior that kept me bound for decades.

When I take a step back and look at my place within the body of Christ, I am amazed. My point in time provides opportunities not available to those who came before. I have unique gifts God has enabled me to develop, and communities I can serve. It's a glimpse at a small part of his grand design.

I may indeed be a drop in the ocean, but the ocean is comprised of drops. They are all needed and collectively they are what forms the ocean. God created each of us with purpose and potential. Through life's ups and downs and the decisions made along the way, you have reached this point today as the person you are. Maybe you've seen some of God's transformative power already. But there is more to come. When we allow God's power into our lives, he transforms us into a new creation designed to fulfill a unique role in his grand redemptive story.

Take some time for inner reflection on the power at work within you. What has God done in your life up to this point and what do you still need to surrender to his transformative power?

All powerful God,

Thank you for the majestic world you have created. Help me to submit to your power at work within me. Transform my life into a creation to be used for your glory. When I feel insignificant, send your Spirit to remind me that you have placed me where I am, as I am, to make a splash for you that ripples throughout the world—always and only for your glory.

Amen.

“

....
....
....
....
....
....
....
....
....
....
....
....
....
....

Temptation in a Teapot

by Patricia Butler

. . . honor God with your bodies.

1 Corinthians 6:20

What do you do when you wake up with a fever, congestion, minor ache, or pain?

Do you reach for the medicine cabinet or inquire of the Lord in prayer?

One morning when I woke with a scratchy throat, I did a little bit of both. I think. Skipping over pleasantries, such as, "Good morning," I threw back the covers and declared, "We'll just nip this in the bud—right, Lord?"

Not exactly inquiring of the Lord. Was it even a prayer?

Stumbling into the bathroom, I rummaged through the medicine cabinet for pain relievers, cold tablets, or throat lozenges. Nothing. Small wonder—after God dramatically healed me of a disability, I'd thrown all my drugs out and rarely stocked medicine anymore. Feeling invincible, I relied on Jehovah-Rapha, my protector, to keep me from all harm. With a fair bit of presumption and growing pride, I practically dared Satan to afflict me again after God's powerful intervention.

So why did I now reach for pills this morning instead of his counsel?

Maybe gargling with salt would work—my mother's old trick. Yes, God certainly didn't want me swallowing unhealthy chemicals. Rubbing my throat (laying on of hands?), I headed for the kitchen, where I spotted my red square teapot. Staring at it in the sink, I remembered last night's ritual: a cup of herbal tea before bed. Lately I'd been drinking too much, and my throat had been complaining.

Last night, a warning also sounded in my spirit, which I ignored. Call it petulance, pride, or self-indulgence—I wanted my tea. I silenced the alarm bells and poured myself a third cup.

"That attitude is the source of your sore throat," the Spirit whispered. "Since you ignored your body and my Spirit, I thought a sore throat would capture your attention."

Guilty as charged. I rinsed the teapot, put the salt away, and swallowed my pride. Apologizing to God, I resolved to moderate my tea consumption in the future. My throat pain disappeared.

To this day, when I overdo it on the tea, I remember that morning and its lessons. Herbal tea can irritate my throat. Honor your body. Listen to its warning signals. Everything in moderation. And when God nudges, stop, look, and listen.

Now I'm glad the medicine chest was empty, so God could adjust my attitude and tune my spiritual ears. When I honor my body and consult him first, I avoid scratchy throats, medical bills, and trips to the pharmacy or doctor's office. No matter our complaint, our Great Physician has a prescription.

When you wake up with a minor ache or pain, what's your

first stop—the medicine cabinet or prayer?

Lord, May my medicine cabinet be an altar of remembrance—where I ask you for the source of my pain and your solution. When I reach for the teapot, may I remember your voice and your goodness. May I honor you with my body and be faithful in the small things. Even a cup of tea. Amen.

“

....
....
....
....
....
....
....
....
....
....
....
....
....
....

God's Eternal Power

by Leigh-Anne Burley

Steadfast love and faithfulness meet;
righteousness and peace kiss each other.

Psalm 85:10 (ESV)

No one wants to hear there is no medical cure; you will never get better, only worse. A cold, wet blanket enveloped my helplessness and hopelessness. A virus had penetrated my heart, leaving permanent scar tissue and damaging the apex. Now my heart did not pump blood efficiently. Disbelief and panic commingled with the dire pronouncement of a limited lifespan. Death became real and I felt alone.

Prior to diagnosis, I knew something was amiss when I got short of breath while walking, and I found climbing stairs challenging. Fatigue settled in like an annoying intruder. At first, I was too stunned to pray, so I asked others to pray. When the shock wore off, I prayed, "Jesus please heal me." However, I wasn't getting better, only worse. I clung to the impression from God that I was not going to die from this.

Jesus understands our fragile faith when presented with perplexing and devastating news. His compassionate heart leans into our profound disappointment and heartache. I became increasingly aware of his caring concern about all facets of my life. At times, it feels like we walk alone, but God is faithful in revealing his abiding presence, comforting and holding us within his accepting embrace.

On the eve of Yom Kippur, I attended my messianic synagogue. Since the building isn't on ground level and there are steep stairs to ascend, I usually could manage if I rested halfway up and recovered in a pew. However, the shortness of breath lingered. At the end of the service, my rabbi said he felt impressed that God wants to heal some people. I certainly was a candidate, so my husband and I went forward for prayer with the rabbi and his wife. The rabbi read in Ezekiel 36:26, where God says, "I will remove the heart of stone from your flesh and give you a heart of flesh" (Ezekiel 36:26 esv).

The scar tissue did feel like stone when it came to pumping blood. I didn't have strong faith going into these prayers, nor did I feel any better right after. However, a few weeks later, I noticed I could walk farther with more air. Soon my distance gradually increased and breathing became easier. I felt brave enough to climb the stairs in my apartment building. At first try, I was somewhat out of breath, but I could make it up to the second floor without resting. Soon I could climb the stairs normally. Eventually, shortness of breath and fatigue dissipated.

Later on, my cardiologist ordered a second sonogram test, which revealed a normally functioning heart. Recently, when flying longer distances with shorter times between connections, I smiled and thanked Jesus for his healing power as I dashed to catch my plane.

It is scary when we don't know the outcome or even the process to go through. We are not guaranteed healing, but we can be confident Jesus loves us intimately and intensely. God's steadfast power guides and comforts us in all trials. Through and in all things, he will never leave or forsake us. The good news is we are never alone.

Whatever your circumstances, do you know that God is right here holding your heart when you are shattered in pieces?

Thank you, Father, that you are indeed a true friend in all our needs, no matter how desperate. You draw close to the brokenhearted, mending and restoring us within your lovingkindness. Jesus, please let those who are hurting and despondent feel the engaging warmth of your presence and experience your power to console all those who mourn.

"

....

....

....

....

....

....

....

....

....

....

....

....

....

....

When We Cannot See the Future

by Linda Summerford

"Never will I leave you;
never will I forsake you."

Hebrews 13:5 (NIV)

Beep, beep, beep. The endless sound of the heart monitor was so loud it was deafening. My sweet husband, Mickey, lay in his hospital bed conscious but with eyes closed.

He had been on the registry for four years due to a lung disease. We had been here in the hospital for a week awaiting his double lung transplant. Dr. Smith would be performing the surgery for one lung and Dr. Myers for the other lung, simultaneously.

"Prep him right now. The lungs are here." Dr. Myers shouted. I jumped up from my chair when I heard those words, my heart pounding in my chest. I grabbed Mickey's hand and began quoting our favorite verse from Hebrews to him.

"Remember, he will never leave you or forsake you." I whispered. Our eyes met and he smiled up at me, tears running down his cheeks, then he was rolled away.

I retreated to the waiting room and opened my Bible to Hebrews 13:5. Mickey was now in God's hands. Hours went by as I waited for a word from the nurse.

"Martha, Martha." I heard someone calling my name and I felt a hand on my shoulder.

Dr. Myers was smiling. "He's doing fine, Martha. He made it through the surgery."

Before I knew it, I had wrapped my arms around the doctor's neck and was sobbing.

Dr. Myers told me what to expect the first time I saw Mickey after surgery as I may not recognize him. There were tubes everywhere. The ventilator moved up and down and his heart monitor beeped. He could not speak because he was in an induced coma. I wanted so badly to let him know I was here, but all I could do was hold his hand and cry.

It was so fitting that the donor of Mickey's lungs was a young man who died while in prison. Mickey had always had a soft spot in his heart for the homeless and those in prison. We had visited the prison many times together to minister to them.

The double-lung transplant was a success. Mickey clung to that verse in Hebrews, especially as he recovered from surgery. He always told me that he would be okay if God called him home. He also wanted me to remember that God would always be with me. But God was not finished with Mickey. He still had things for Mickey to do.

Do you know today that God will never leave you nor forsake you?

Lord, when we must accept that we cannot see what our future holds, but we know that you can see the big picture, help us to always remember your promise to never leave us or forsake us.

"

....
....
....
....
....
....
....
....
....
....
....
....
....
....

God is Near

by L.B. Snider

The Lord is near to the brokenhearted and saves the crushed in spirit.

Psalm 34:18 (ESV)

As young as fourteen, I knew something wrong with me, but I didn't know what it was nor how to fix myself. I related to Humpty Dumpty; all the king's men couldn't put me back together again, no matter how hard they tried. There were too many jagged, broken, and missing puzzle pieces inside of me.

The accurate diagnosis would come decades later. Dissociative identity disorder (DID), more commonly known as multiple personality disorder, is caused by experiencing severe and sustained abuse at a young age. I struggled with anxiety, depression, disorientation, and detachment as an adult. My recovery was a decade-long and painful process that involved talking with qualified therapists concerning my repressed memories of the traumas.

My parents conditioned me to identify myself from a young age as an innately inadequate and worthless person that no one could ever love. Over the years, God's unfailing faithfulness and unconditional love revealed that I am his beloved precious daughter. The Holy Spirit, through his Word and his presence, whispers that I am wanted and loved. God's continuous loving-kindness radiates from heaven into my thirsty soul, esteeming and valuing me beyond measure.

The enemy of my soul weakened my mind with darkness, disorder, and chaos, but through Jesus' transforming power and love, I possess a sound mind. My fragile soul no longer resides in sinking sand but is forever established in God's solid foundation through his inerrant Word. Once adrift in a sea of turmoil, my volatile emotions are now anchored in God's true wisdom. I am no longer detached because I am securely attached to the Vine with his life flowing through my veins. Caregivers in my family of origin eventually abandoned and forsook their children, but Christ, the good Shepherd, found and hugged me closer. No longer a forgotten child, I am adopted into the family of God. Instead of enduring panic attacks, now the Prince of Peace calms my mind and gathers me like a tender mother hiding me under the shadow of her wings.

When others in my recovery judged and left me, my Savior constantly stayed by my side, encouraging me to be brave by trusting in his unfailing goodness. Jesus quelled my outrage and anger by leading me onto the rocky and thorny path of forgiveness. He picked me up while his sustaining mercies gave me hope in his name. He is a faithful friend who is always near in times of trouble, binding up the wounds interwoven and stitched into my shattered heart. Heaven shines throughout my life, causing me to rejoice in the goodness of God. Satan is the stealer of our joy. Jesus is the healer who brings beauty out of ashes. His strong right arm rescued an impoverished prisoner locked in the kingdom of darkness and translated me into the realm of his marvelous light. Jesus's sacrifice brought heaven to earth. He sees me for who I am in him. His eternal kindness embraces us right where we are, bringing us closer to his never-ending kingdom of light. In the eyes of a merciful God, there are no worthless or hopeless cases because Jesus liberates and celebrates our lives in him.

God is loving and kind, caring deeply about every detail of our lives. Our Lord graciously invites us to walk and talk with him as his children as he leads us in our healing process by conforming us into his image. What do you need to take to the Lord today?

God, Scriptures declare you are near to the brokenhearted and save the crushed in spirit. Your gracious presence welcomes all into your loving and accepting embrace. Thank you for your sacrifice through your son so we may walk in his perfect purchased freedom and light. You set the captives free from the power of darkness and usher them into your Kingdom of light. May you be glorified today. Amen.

“

....
....
....
....
....
....
....
....
....
....
....
....
....
....

My Traumatic Stroke

By Lori Vober

Many are the plans in a person's heart,
but it is the Lord's purpose that prevails

Proverbs 19:21 (NIV)

January 26, 2003 was a typical cold, snowy day in Minnesota, and I had just started my new position as the office manager at our church three weeks prior. A month earlier, I would have been in my corporate sales job at the airlines, possibly on an airplane.

It was a Friday and usually I work alone on Fridays. This particular day, there was a coworker working in the office with me and a women's Bible study going on down the hall when I started to feel sick. I was only 29 years old and very healthy, so I did not think anything huge was wrong until suddenly my left arm felt heavy and then my left leg went numb. I did not realize it at the time, but I was having a massive stroke. I would later learn that I'd had an intracerebral hemorrhagic stroke caused by an undetected malformation of blood vessels on the right side of my brain.

God's hand of protection and unfailing faithfulness was over me that terrible day. I thought I was making a career change from the airlines to the church to lessen our stress load and help our family planning. However, I now believe the job change was to save my life. In addition, it was a miracle I was not alone at the church that day.

Upon arriving at the hospital, I underwent a five-hour emergency brain surgery to stop the bleeding and woke up seventeen days later from a drug-induced coma, paralyzed on the left side. After a second ten-hour brain surgery to remove the malformation, I went home in a wheelchair after two months in the hospital. In an instant, my life had changed.

A few months after my hospital discharge, another challenge hit our family when my husband lost his job in the aviation industry. He found a new one, and we relocated to Arizona. Again, God's faithfulness was upon us, and we are so thankful that through our challenges we have been able to persevere with a strong faith, knowing God is by our side. I found a wonderful new neurotherapy clinic in Arizona and was one of their first patients. I would never have recovered and be where I am today had it not been for this therapy clinic.

I worked for years at therapy, treating it like my full-time job, in order to get my independence back. Eight years post stroke, we continued with our family planning and internationally adopted a sibling group of three. I recently became an author and published my first book to share my story and help others. Many times throughout the years I have had a plan in mind, but I have learned to keep my eyes on God for the best plan and trust in his purpose.

Have you or a loved one ever experienced a serious medical issue or life-altering change in plans, and if so, how did you handle it?

Dear God, whenever our original plans don't work out, please remind us to thank you and look to you for guidance. Many times our plans don't work out because your plan is bigger and better. Help us to have a strong faith in you so that we can be in tune to know what your plan is for us. Thank you for taking care of your children. Amen.

“

....
....
....
....
....
....
....
....
....
....
....
....
....
....

Upheld by God's Faithfulness

by Norma Poore

Do not fear, for I am with you; Do not anxiously look about you, for I am your God. I will strengthen you, surely I will help you, Surely I will uphold you with My righteous right hand.

Isaiah 41:10 (NASB)

The doctor said "You have pneumonia and need to be admitted" Like pinballs in an arcade game not able to land in the winning spot, these words rolled around my brain with no place to stop. Three days before this, my cousin died from being on a ventilator due to pneumonia and here I was in the hospital for the same thing.

My eyes locked with my husband's. He and I have endured many hardships over the forty years since we exchanged our vows. Now, concern and fear covered his face. "Go on home, honey. You don't need to sleep here tonight. I'll be fine. I love you." And with that, he blew me a kiss and left.

The hum of machines attached to me, shuffling feet and quiet whispers from the hall were welcomed distractions from the thoughts raging in my head. So many sick and dying. Anxiety gripped me. Will I be next?

I wasn't afraid of dying, but of not being there for my family. Not able to help my daughter with her newborn or to support my sons. I wouldn't be able to see my grandchildren grow up. And who will be there to advocate for my special needs son?

A sob caught in my throat. Tears cascaded.

Help me, God. I'm scared. I don't want to die. I'm so alone. Where are you? Please help!

Sleep faded in and out. I was haunted by thoughts of death and never seeing friends and loved ones again on earth.

"Good morning." The nurse said. I wasn't so sure. Her words didn't make me feel better. I preferred to go back to sleep, since I had so little of it. Curtains opened. Bright sunshine lit my room, but I wasn't sure it belonged here in a situation like this.

One by one, verses from God's Word came to mind.

"Be still and know that I am God" (Psalm 46:10).

"Surely I will help you. Surely I will uphold you with my righteous right hand" (Isaiah 41:10).

"The Lord is the one who goes ahead of you. He will not forsake you. Do not fear" (Deuteronomy 31:8).

Memorized Scripture penetrated my brain fog, brought light to my soul, and reminded me that God is in control. If I die, he'll take good care of my family and heal their broken hearts.

Peace settled on me like a warm blanket. I slept well that night. Four days later, I went home with two oxygen tanks, happy to know God wasn't finished with me yet.

I anxiously looked at the fearful situation surrounding me. But God showed his faithfulness, strengthened me, and upheld me with his righteous right hand.

Whether you face illness, the death of a loved one, financial trouble, or maybe a deep heartache for wayward children, God sees you. He hears your cries and will show his unfailing faithfulness to you while holding you in his righteous right hand.

What is preventing you from experiencing God's unfailing faithfulness?

Father, thank you for answering my prayer. Strengthen those, like me, who struggle with fear. Show us that we don't have to be anxious and afraid, but can bring our biggest fears or smallest problems to you with thanksgiving, knowing you will hear us and give peace that passes all understanding, which guards our hearts and minds like it says in Philippians. Thank you for your unfailing faithfulness. In Jesus's name. Amen.

"

....
....
....
....
....
....
....
....
....
....
....
....
....
....

Contradictions

by Ann Griffiths

For the Lord is good; his steadfast love endures forever,
and his faithfulness to all generations.

Psalm 100:5 (ESV)

Heavy, humid air hung thick with unfriendly odors that flooded the dirty, dilapidated room where we were told to stand and wait. The walls no longer held color, if ever there was color, and the remaining strips of peeling paint exposed pock-marked cement walls. A sad history of generations, past and present, seemed to linger in the room's dim lighting.

To my right, I caught a glimpse of a woman peeking out from behind a door. She held a baby in her arms while six tiny, unkempt children huddled around her. Their blank faces revealed nothing, yet their demeanor spoke volumes. To these lost and forgotten children, this desolate overseas orphanage was home.

In stark contrast to our meager surroundings, a line of small children entered the room from the left of where we stood. It looked like they were specially chosen, washed, and dressed in clean, crisp clothes to perform for the foreigners. As they took their places in front of us, some stared at the floor while others ventured a glance in our direction. After an official gave a brief introduction, the children began to sing. And, as if on cue, they smiled.

My heart and head struggled to make sense of this place. Singing voices contradicted stoic expressions. Sweet sounds competed with sour smells. And the innocent beauty of small faces challenged the battered décor of reality.

When we walked out of the room and made our way along the alley outside, I turned back toward the compound. A young boy stood alone at the top of the three stairs leading to the building, and his eyes followed us. Watching. Alone. Abandoned.

Did he think of us as unwelcome intruders? Did he wear an invisible mask of longing, or one of contempt? Did he see compassion in that moment of time when I looked back and our eyes met? Only God knows.

Contradictions and unknowns fill our lives. We cry when we lose a loved one; and we laugh with friends and family. We battle the storms of life and bask in the stillness of a sun-soaked lake. We endure disappointments and celebrate victories.

Yet through all of life's journey, God is sovereign. When we are insecure, he is steadfast. When we are unfaithful, he is faithful. When we deserve judgment, he offers grace and mercy.

Like that young boy, you may feel alone or abandoned. Or maybe you're uncertain about life or a pending outcome. Know this: God is faithful. God is good. God is sovereign.

I don't know what happened to that boy who stood alone on the step, but God knows. He is faithful to all generations and across all nations. His love extends to that boy and to you, because God is love. When you feel lonely, or sit crying, or stand waiting, know that his faithfulness is true. God is not a contradiction. He does not mask his reality. He is love and mercy. He is good and faithful.

What do you need to let go of and trust to God's sovereign faithfulness?

Father in Heaven, thank you for your faithfulness throughout my life, even when life was messy. Thank you for your goodness and love to my family and for generations to come. In today's uncertain time, help me rest in your sovereign will and focus on you. In Jesus' name. Amen.

"

....
....
....
....
....
....
....
....
....
....
....
....
....
....

Always Have Hope: Really?

by Heather MacAskill

As for me, I will always have hope;
I will praise you more and more.

Psalm 71:14 (NIV)

The words flew at me, unexpected and loaded with pain. "Brain tumor." "Stage 4." "Metastatic." I tried desperately to process. I glanced at the phone where I knew my husband was listening at the other end. Covid restrictions had required him to stay in the car. I was alone. What was happening? How could this be? While my mind desperately flailed around, trying to make sense of all that was coming at me, one more phrase filled the room. "Get your affairs in order."

Like a final knockout blow, those words were a gut punch. They sucked the hope out of my world.

The psalmist makes a bold claim. "But as for me, I will always have hope" (Psalm 71:14, NIV). Always? Even after a horrible diagnosis? In the days, weeks, and months that followed my diagnosis, I had a choice to make. I could choose to live in the darkness that comes when hope is gone, or I could actively search for hope. I didn't like what the darkness was bringing, so

I cried out to Jesus. I dove into my Bible, searching for answers. My need was huge—all consuming. It was hard work. Every day the battle raged, and the choice was before me.

Jesus was there, holding the hope I desperately needed. In order to grab that hope, I had to let go of what was in my hands: the fear, the uncertainty, the pain. Jesus was so sweet during that time. He lovingly, sweetly, showed me how to loosen my grip and surrender everything to him.

As I did, he replaced fear and pain with hope. The more I surrendered, the more hope grew. It wasn't alone though. As the hope grew, praise came right alongside it. I could never imagine being able to praise God during such terrible circumstances. It was Jesus at work in me, his spirit transforming me.

"But as for me, I will always have hope; I will praise you more and more" (Psalm 71:14 NIV). What a marvelous work Jesus offers us. When we surrender all of the fear and pain to him, he replaces it with hope, and our spirits are lightened and filled with praise. Only Jesus could bring that kind of transformation. It was more than I could have imagined.

Jesus brings the same offer of transformation to you. This is not some positive thinking ideology. The exchange of fear and pain for hope and praise is a powerful work of the Holy Spirit. It's not something we can do ourselves. It's a gift, given by a loving Jesus. He doesn't leave us in our fear and pain. He comes alongside us, making an amazing offer to replace the fear and pain with hope and praise. Our surrender allows him to make this powerful transformation.

What is Jesus asking you to surrender to Him today?

Jesus, thank you for walking with us through the circumstances of life. The sweet gift of transformation is something only you can do. Show us today what we need to let go of and lay at your feet. Take the fear and pain, and by your Holy Spirit, replace it with hope and praise. In Jesus' name, amen.

“

....
....
....
....
....
....
....
....
....
....
....
....
....
....

God's Abundant Kindness

by Jenn Dafoe-Turner

Trust in the Lord with all your heart; do not depend on your own understanding. Seek his will in all you do, and he will show you which path to take.

Proverbs 3:5-6 (NLT)

I lay with my eyes closed, sinking into the sofa's cushions. Soft worship music played while I waited for the Lord to speak to my heart. So many thoughts ran through my newly sober mind as I took a break from writing my memoir. The heaviness of remembering weighed on me, and I longed to be refreshed.

Soon into my thoughts, the Holy Spirit gripped me with a vision of my house. He began to walk me through it. In the kitchen, he said, "See, you let me settle here." Then to the living room, he said, "See, you let me settle here." Then to the bathroom, he said, "See, you let me settle here." Then to the bedroom, he said, "See, you haven't let me settle here."

I cried out, "Lord, please forgive me. Settle in the places I haven't let you. I need you." I thought I had surrendered and allowed the Lord to settle over every area of my life.

However, the fullness of surrender didn't happen until I was on a mission trip to Cuba a few years later. While I was there, the mission leader was in prayer over me, and the Lord gave him a vision. He described it, saying, "I see you standing before God's throne. You are wrapped in black. Something is blocking what the Lord is trying to do in you so he can act through you."

Later, in the solitude of my room, I journaled about what the leader shared. In the kindest way possible, the Holy Spirit said, "Jenn, my daughter, I was with you when you walked through the fires of addiction. When you walked the journey of recovery, I was with you. When you moved to Prince Edward Island, I made the way. When you needed work, I provided four jobs. I gave you seventy-seven acres with a farm and house when you had no home. When you had absolutely nothing but me, I came through."

I was undone in the presence of my Lord.

I realized how much the blackness of distrust enveloped me. Could God be trusted? In the past, I became so angry with God because I trusted him so much and felt as if he had let me down. I thought I had lost everything. But the reality was, I walked away. I chose to carry the burdens. I decided not to journey through the pain and heartache to a place of wholeness and healing. Yet, God never abandoned me. He never forsook me. I believed the enemy's lies instead of the truth of God's words. I chose to let my feelings rule my heart instead of God's truth.

God transformed my trust in him. I received holy help. I will not face another situation without him. God is faithful. If we let him settle in the private areas, he will continually transform our faith in his faithfulness. Will you?

Spend time with the Holy Spirit. Where have you seen

God's faithfulness, and where have you not yet let God settle? Reflect on your trust relationship with our Father and where it could use some holy help.

Father in Heaven, thank you for your abundant kindness. Thank you for loving us with grace and mercy. Would you show us areas of our lives where we may be walking in our own strength or not trusting in you or your provision? Lord, you are the Great I Am, and we can trust the one who created us to remind us when we forget. In Jesus' name, amen.

“

....
....
....
....
....
....
....
....
....
....
....
....
....
....

Seed of Faith

by Susanne Moore

Oh give thanks to the Lord; call upon his name; make known his deeds among the peoples!

I Chronicles 16:8 (ESV)

The daily grind of monotonous phone calling, emailing, and texting was driving my weary soul into a negative spiral of thoughts. After thirty-three years of building relationships with my customers, I can easily become frustrated with the new electronic age of communication, not only with my customers but also with my staff.

When this happens, I take a mental hiatus, say a little prayer, and set my heart back on solid ground. God is incredibly faithful in restarting my engine towards serving others. Usually this is with little reminders of why I do what I do—to plant seeds and share my faith.

The other day, I received a phone call from a former employee who had now become his own agent. We caught up on our families and how business was going. Then he told me he was missing something in his life, and he had been trying to figure it out. He had recently spoken with my boss, who had directed him to church, but hadn't taken the time to go. He asked me if I had any devotionals I thought would empower him to move.

"The Bible would be my first answer; have you ever read it?"

He chuckled a little and confessed, "I have attempted it a few times, but I just do not understand it."

Inwardly, I had that leap in my spirit and I asked him if he had a Bible. We talked for a long time about different versions of Scripture, and about how to get him a Spanish translation with commentary, table of contents, and so on.

Truly, I was excited to have some direction on how I could bless him. I missed him as an employee because he was dedicated and always such a joy to have around with his contagious laugh. He always sang mariachi at our Christmas parties. Mental note: invite him to our Christmas party this year.

As we were gearing down to say goodbye, he said, "Wait. Do you remember the first day I came to work for you? Do you remember what you said to me?"

I confessed I did not.

He laughed heartily. "You said, 'well, are you coming back tomorrow?' That has stuck with me all these years. When I am having a bad day at the office, I ask myself, 'Well, are you coming back tomorrow?' That really encouraged me. I also miss prayers before our meetings; it always blessed me that we prayed."

Those little seeds of faith, planted years ago, were coming to fruition. Wow, God!

When we plant, God fertilizes and grows those seeds deep inside someone's heart. This confession grew hope in my own soul, reminding me that God's words, as well as the way we live our life and speak to others, is a testimony of God's faithfulness to water and grow other people's faith too.

In the daily grind of living your life, have you witnessed the growth from the seeds you planted for Jesus?

Jesus, sometimes we fall into a negative thought pattern that leads us away from the calling you have placed on our lives. Thank you for the gentle reminders that you are watering and growing those seeds where we planted them. It, in turn, helps us grow in our faith. Lead us forward and keep us planting words of encouragement and truth into people we encounter every day.

“

....
....
....
....
....
....
....
....
....
....
....
....
....
....

Seeing God in My Shrunken Life

by Dianne Barker

It is the Lord: let him do what seemeth him good.

1 Samuel 3:18 (KJV)

Caught in the "sandwich generation," rearing two children while caring for aging parents, I often felt overwhelmed and discouraged.

A devotional by Hannah Whitall Smith in the Streams in the Desert (Cowman 1925, 271-272) highlighted 1 Samuel 3:18. She said if we try to see God in everything, He will calm and color everything we see.

How could anyone see God in wars and calamities causing suffering and heartbreak worldwide? In challenges and setbacks assaulting my life?

The writer said circumstances may not change, but seeing Christ in them changes us. Seeing Him in our situation, confident He makes no mistakes, allows us to bless His name whatever comes. This perspective, she said, would make us loving and patient with people who annoy us and enable us to stop our murmuring.

At the time, I was prone to murmuring. Having our two

children born just nineteen months apart introduced me to an unforeseen reality—sibling rivalry. Those precious little people had strong personalities, creating frequent conflict. Although I loved them desperately, I responded in anger, feeling like a parenting failure.

Caring for my parents and my husband's parents added more stress. Three of my four siblings lived out of state. My nearby brother helped, but because of serious health issues, he also needed my assistance. My husband, an only child, had no help as his parents declined.

A successful journalist and best-selling author, I found myself in a place I call the shrunken life. The Lord had eliminated every non-essential thing, shrinking my life to basics: driving our parents to appointments, going to school functions, attending church, shopping for groceries, and household chores for our three families. The idea of seeing God in everything seemed radical.

Ms. Smith's book, The Christian's Secret of a Happy Life (Smith 1970, 101-102), introduced another extreme concept—accepting everything as coming directly from God's hand. The author acknowledged thoughtless people cause most of our difficulties, but accepting the wound as coming from God's hand brings sweet consolation. She said since our Father controls all second causes, these come to us only if He knows and permits them. I learned to look for God's hand in my shrunken life and soon noticed an unexplainable peace and joy.

Growing up takes time—and so does growing in Christlikeness. At times I've felt like a toddler, spending more time on the ground than on foot, wrestling to apply those principles. When I struggled to find purpose, I'd remember: This trial passed through the hands of my loving Father. There's no second cause. God has a purpose. I needn't see it to believe it.

These many years later, am I always loving and patient? Have I stopped all murmuring? I'm making progress. I find yielding each experience to God, accepting it from His hand, indeed brings sweet consolation. My Father has proven himself absolutely trustworthy!

In a baffling circumstance that caused you to question God's purpose, how did He speak peace to your troubled heart?

Father, I know I can trust you. And that settles everything. Whatever life brings, I choose to remember that you love me and have a purpose in whatever you allow to touch my life. When my faith wavers, remind me you will use this circumstance for my good and your glory as I press forward, praising your holy name. You are the Lord. Do what seems good to you.

"

....
....
....
....
....
....
....
....
....
....
....
....
....
....

Stranger Danger

by Roberta Sarver

The angel of the Lord encampeth round about them that fear him, and delivereth them.

Psalm 34:7 (KJV)

Jeanand a friend, both teachers at their rural school, attended a church convention. They arrived eager to hear sermons and music, and connect with old friends from around the nation.

Partway through the afternoon, Jean volunteered to trek back to the car to feed the parking meter. That's when she almost became a kidnapping victim.

"Nice day, isn't it?"

Jean looked up to see who was speaking. Next to her stood a middle-aged woman wearing heavy makeup, an expensive dress, and a mink stole.

"Oh, sure is," said Jean.

"Well, aren't you the prettiest thing!" the strange woman cooed. "What are you doing here in Huntington, Sweetie?"

"A friend and I came from Virginia to attend a church

convention," answered Jean.

"Well, you're far away from home, aren't you?"

"I guess so."

"I've just never seen someone so pretty and wholesome before," purred the stranger. "Would you like to see where I live? It's right there in that store." The woman led Jean into a large jewelry store and introduced her to the man behind the counter.

"And I live up those stairs," she motioned to the bewildered girl. Jean turned and stared at a grand staircase. An elegant mahogany door stood at the top. Why would someone live in a jewelry store?

Suddenly Jean felt an impending sense of evil. What was behind that door? And why did she feel she would be trapped if she entered it? "Well, I really need to get back to the convention," she said.

"Here, let me give you my address," the stranger spoke as she wrote on a scrap of paper. "You really are a pretty little thing. Be sure and write to me."

A few weeks later, Jean sent the stranger a letter. Thinking the woman had never seen someone untainted by a wild lifestyle, Jean intended to develop a correspondence. This would give her a chance to tell her about the Savior, the One who could give everyone a better way of living. The letter was returned and marked "Undeliverable."

Becoming older and wiser, Jean realized she had been given a false address by a criminal posing as a friendly woman on the street. No doubt the stranger was running a house of prostitution, luring girls for her "business." One step through the mahogany door would have meant walking into a trap.

Discerning evil is one of the gifts God gives his children. It worked that day for an otherwise trusting young adult and will work for anyone walking in God's light.

How do I know? I was Jean.

Did you ever sense danger and later learn what it was? You and I can thank God he sends his angels to guard us in our unguarded moments.

Dear Heavenly Father, thank you for the gift of discernment. Please make us wise as serpents and harmless as doves as we inhabit a world steeped in evil. Keep us like the lily at the mouth of a coal mine, clean and unspotted by the filth around us. In Christ's name, amen.

"

....
....
....
....
....
....
....
....
....
....
....
....
....
....

Rescued by God

by Joylin Lane

He brought me out of the miry clay, and set my feet upon a rock. He has put a new song in my mouth…

Psalm 40:2-3 (NKJV)

I could never imagine such an experience, nor could I conceive of ever recovering from such a tragedy. But the greatest loss a parent can experience happened the day my son Matthew died. He was just twenty-seven. Like Rachel in Jeremiah 31:15, I refused to be comforted. Though others tried, no one understood, and no words could help assuage my grief. Consumed by sorrow, despair was my constant companion. I was cast into an abyss so deep, I felt life was over.

Even though I had two other children and a husband, I found it difficult to function. I wanted to die. My world had stopped, and I couldn't face my incomprehensible reality.

As a Christian I knew only God could save me. I ran to him for refuge. When I couldn't express myself to others, or they couldn't comprehend, I poured out my agony to him. He knew the depth of my mourning, the troubling questions, and the hopelessness I felt.

Years ago in my quest to know him more intimately, I began a routine each month of reading five Psalms and one Proverb a day. Whatever the date, I begin with that number in the Psalms. Then skip thirty, read that Psalm, skip thirty, etc. until all one hundred fifty Psalms are read. I also read the Proverb for that date. This is a regular part of my quiet time with the Lord. It would prove invaluable in preparing me for what lay ahead.

In my grief, I immersed myself in the Psalms. The book is full of laments. As I read, my anguish and misery were validated. Like David I'd cry out, "Lord, help me" as I wailed and wept. Often I'd express my feelings on the pages of my journal, knowing he understood my pain. This was cathartic. God's word became my comfort. I didn't realize this practice would be my lifeline.

In my weakness, I came face to face with my strong and living God. He promised to deliver me from my prison of inconsolable sorrow.

After a few years, I slowly began to emerge from the dark valley as a result of his intervention. Restoration, according to the dictionary, is "returning something to a former condition." Could I recover from such a devastating loss? In my mind, that was an impossibility. But God surprised me by enabling me to process my grief through writing out what I learned from Scripture. I'm amazed at how far I've come.

As a new believer in Christ, I chose Psalm 40:2-3 as my life verse. "He brought me out of the miry clay, and set my feet upon a rock. He has put a new song in my mouth…" Initially, this verse spoke to me of my salvation, but it took on greater meaning as I was engulfed in grief. God rescued me a second time by his transforming power. He brought me from death to life.

Through my struggle he revealed his love, concern, and attention to my needs. When I couldn't walk, he carried me and gently guided me back to wholeness. He is restoring my soul and has promised that I would see the "goodness of the Lord in the land of the living" (Psalm 27:13).

Can you trust God with your impossible situation? He will meet you in your heartache if you ask for his help.

Father, remind me that when I am weak, you are strong. Help me to recognize my need for you in the midst of trials. To run to your word for the comfort, guidance, and support that I need. Keep my eyes on your promises to deliver me. Thank you for your faithfulness.

"

....
....
....
....
....
....
....
....
....
....
....
....
....
....

Divine Dependence

by Kasey Burnett

Trust in the Lord with all your heart
And do not lean on your own understanding.
In all your ways acknowledge Him,
And He will make your paths straight.

Proverbs 3:5-6 (NASB)

As relentlessly as the rainwater seeped through our leaky roof, cancer found its way into our chaos, taking hold of my husband Paul. Everything was falling apart. Nearly every appliance in our home was broken, and the lawn mower wouldn't start. The roof leaked from eight places, and the kitchen floor was peeling. Life became more than either of us could fix.

Settling into our brokenness, the focus became radiation and chemotherapy treatments. Paul had a procedure to get a chemo port and, after a lot of persuasion, the placement of a feeding tube. That year became a time of destruction and despair.

Elijah found God's care during a difficult season in his life. He had exhibited marvelous confidence while confronting wicked King Ahab, declaring a long drought would overcome the land as a sign of God's judgment. Elijah experienced the glory of God and reflected the Almighty's power by acknowledging his sovereignty, and there was no rain. The drought angered the king, so the Lord sent Elijah to hide near a brook. While he was there, the Lord sent ravens to provide meat and bread, morning and night until eventually, the brook dried up.

Then Elijah traveled to a city where the Lord told him a widow would provide for him. He asked her for a little water and a piece of bread. But the widow had no bread, and with her exhausted supplies, she planned to prepare the last meal for her son and herself. She expected they'd die.

Elijah told the widow not to fear. He sent her to make bread for him, and then to go make some for her and her son. His request was a call to faith with a promise of life. Her response was acknowledgment of the Living God, and she received impossible provisions until the rain came.

Life as we knew it was on hold. Returning from the new routine of daily treatments, I'd close the bedroom door so Paul could sleep. It was time for me to be Mom again—to check schoolwork, prepare meals, and tend to the family. Daily, I reached for groceries not there and grabbed my purse for a quick trip to the store. Each car ride, a conversation with the Lord released tears and re-established faith.

During one of Paul's radiation treatments, God sent a widow to us. She interrupted my anxious waiting time and filled our van with groceries from her Sunday school class.

Paul and I made new stands with the Living God in our trials. We discovered God's faithfulness to provide for our family for six months when Paul couldn't. His coworkers were like Elijah's ravens, bringing provisions while he was out of work for treatments. They organized a fundraiser and donated their reserved time. Paul never missed a paycheck. If that wasn't enough, they partnered with our church to put a roof on our house. Family and friends helped with chores, money, and encouragement.

God's mercy touched our brokenness one provision at a time. Eventually, Paul was healed from cancer. Learning complete dependence on the Lord proved he is living and active in unimaginable ways—breathing life into the details of our trials and guiding us on the path to his kingdom.

How have your circumstances revealed the Living God in the details of your journey to his kingdom?

Heavenly Father, forgive me when I'm tempted to doubt. Help me to see you more clearly in all things. I need you to guard my heart and lead my way. Thank you for providing for my needs, especially my need for a Savior and an eternal home. Amen.

“

God's Glory through His Church

Practice What is Preached

by Teresa Janzen

Now to him who is able to do immeasurably more than all we ask or imagine, according to his power that is at work within us, to him be glory in the church and in Christ Jesus throughout all generations, for ever and ever! Amen.

Ephesians 3:20-21 (NIV)

Summer camp was the highlight of my childhood social calendar. I knew money was tight in our family, but somehow Mom always found the resources to send me to camp. It's where I made lifelong friends, where I was baptized, and where I learned the songs and scriptures that would carry me through difficult seasons of life. Years later, I learned that scholarships, combined with youth group car washes and whatever money mom could scrape together, funded my yearly adventure.

I always loved the missionary speakers at camp. Their stories were so exciting. One year, at the end of the missionary's presentation, he invited those who wanted to dedicate their lives to ministry to join him up front. My heart pounded. There was no way I could stay in my seat.

When Mom came to pick me up from camp, I told her

about my new vocational calling. Though she never voiced an objection, she later confessed that she had no idea what it meant to be a missionary. All she could imagine was my being cooked by cannibals.

I'll never know the people who contributed their hard-earned money to make a difference in my life, yet I'm grateful for them. How would my life have been different if no one contributed to that scholarship fund? Would I have gone to Bible school or be serving in ministry today? Would I have known how to return to the Lord when my faith was challenged or when I took a zig-zaggy path?

The church is designed to be a place where people are nurtured to grow spiritually. The entire book of Ephesians illustrates what it looks like when transformed individuals worship God in unity—resulting in God being glorified through his church.

In western culture, we tend to endorse the merits of individual behavior, and that certainly is important. Yet the church is a body of unique individuals united by a shared faith in Jesus Christ. While a person can bring glory to God by what he or she does or says, the impact of a unified body exemplifying God's transformative teachings is even more powerful.

God is glorified when the church cares for the vulnerable, teaches children in the ways of the Lord, encourages those who are discouraged, and visits the lonely and outcast. God is also glorified when the church confronts injustice, stands for truth, admonishes evil, and speaks up for those who have no voice.

Francis of Assisi said, "Preach the Gospel at all times, and when necessary use words." In other words, the church is called to not only preach but to practice what is preached.

In what ways is your church congregation glorifying God as a unified body?

Father God, thank you for creating your people to be people in fellowship and unity. Help me to work with others by doing my part and letting other people do their part to show your love, and mercy to others. Amen.

"

....

....

....

....

....

....

....

....

....

....

....

....

....

....

Who Decides If My Life Matters

by Sandra Hastings

For we are his workmanship, created in Christ Jesus unto good works, which God hath before ordained that we should walk in them.

Ephesians 2:10 (KJV)

Most of us want to know what our purpose is and if we can make a difference. But who decides this? Are we the judge, or is society?

Our limited knowledge of the future can make it difficult for us to determine that purpose and the extent of our influence.

According to the world, our value depends on the ability to work and the opinions of others. However, what is acceptable and expected constantly changes from one year to the next, from one generation to the next.

Our master designer, Jesus Christ, made each of us unique. Therefore, he is the only one who knows both what we are created to do and how our life will impact others.

Let's think of it like this. What if a violin wants to play a masterpiece at Carnegie Hall? What if a piece of clay wants to become a beautiful vase in the Oval Office of the White House? Can either accomplish their desire in their own strength or ability? How do they even know that is their intended purpose?

The violin is a musical instrument, but it can only make music in the hands of a musician. A lump of clay is dependent on the potter who controls the wheel. Remember our Designer is the only one who knows how he wants to use our life. We were made dependent on design.

John Newton was a heartless, cruel, slave trader and a shrewd businessman. He lived an evil life with little care or concern for any man. His Designer, however, had a plan. Through events beyond Newton's control, when he thought he was facing death, he cried out to God for help. At that moment grace moved in, Jesus saved his soul, and John was changed. At the age of thirty-nine, Newton was ordained as an Anglican minister and began writing simple, heartfelt hymns. We still sing many of them today.

When Nicholas Vujicic was born his mother refused to hold him. Her son did not have arms or legs and his family struggled with his condition. But in time, they accepted him as God's gift and believed God had a plan for his life. Today, Nicholas is a world-renowned motivational speaker and shares his faith with millions of people. His unique difference makes him a compelling witness for Christ.

Our society would not have considered these well-known people to be valuable, yet they made a significant impact on the world.

So, back to our original question. Does your life matter and who decides? Most definitely—your life matters! Don't determine your personal worth by what others say. Look to the

One who designed you and loves you unconditionally. Accept who you are in Christ and by faith, fulfill your destiny.

What are you basing your self-worth on?

Dear Lord, Help me to see my value in you and not through the eyes of this world. Help me to accept myself as I am knowing you made me for a purpose and to bring you glory. Thank you, Lord, that I can trust you to show me through your Word and the Holy Spirit what you want me to do. I love you, Lord. Amen

“

....
....
....
....
....
....
....
....
....
....
....
....
....
....

Good News!

by Leann Seale

For we are God's handiwork, created in Christ Jesus to do good works, which God prepared in advance for us to do.

Ephesians 2:10 (NIV)

It was a new season. My four boys were well into their first year of public school after being homeschooled. I was in a low place, tired of making lunches, rushing to soccer practices, helping with homework—the mundane.

As I look back, I can see that I needed purpose in my life. I decided to pray and ask God to show me where he would like me to serve him now that my boys were in school. Just four days later, at women's Bible study, a speaker talked to us about after-school Christian clubs at public elementary schools. She had started clubs in the neighboring city and was asking for someone to start a club in our town.

My first thought was, "Wow, God works fast!" Then I thought, "Oh no, not me!" Launching a new club meant obtaining school district approval, organizing and planning with the principal and staff, coordinating volunteers, and gathering students to attend. So I decided I would pray about it. That was safe.

So I prayed . . . all that summer. Then fall hit, the busiest time for our family to date. We had a whiteboard that hung in our kitchen with all of the boys' activities. It was full each day.

Then one Sunday during a sermon, our pastor was talking about service and furthering the kingdom of heaven on earth. I was taking notes. How exactly should I serve?

Our pastor kept repeating, "Go and teach the good news of Jesus." He must have said these words fifteen times. Finally, it clicked, and I wrote down, "Good News Clubs!" I felt like all of the angels in heaven were cheering that I got the message, and I wanted to laugh and cry at the same time. There was no doubt about the clarity I had from God as I sat in shock and excitement.

God confirmed that he was working when one of our pastors said he had been praying for two years for a parent to start such a club and our church would sponsor the club. Praying and relying on God's leading, I kept hearing God's nudging to: "Go big! Plan for a large club, and I will bring the children." Most clubs meet in a classroom with 15-30 students. I requested the use of our cafeteria, knowing we would need the space.

By the time everything was in place, it was January, and our family whiteboard was empty. Our first club had 85 students in attendance. Our Good News Club soon grew to become one of the largest in the United States, with many students making first-time commitments to follow Jesus.

God illuminated Ephesians 2:10, showing me that he graciously calls us into kingdom work, which he orchestrates. If willing, we get the privilege of working with God himself.

Partnering with the one who provides above and beyond our imagination is exhilarating work.

Do you feel God nudging you into kingdom work? Fasten your seatbelt and commit your time and energy to the Lord. In God's economy, you will be blessed beyond measure.

Dear Heavenly Father, I am humbled and in awe of the way you work. You don't need me; you are Creator of heaven and earth, yet you prepare works in advance, so that I may join you. Praise you that you choose to allow me, a broken vessel, to serve with you. You teach me to listen and follow you, growing my faith and devotion. Thank you for your ways. In Jesus' name, amen.

"

....

....

....

....

....

....

....

....

....

....

....

....

....

....

The Anchor in My Storm

by Betty A Rodgers-Kulich

This hope we have as an anchor of the soul, both sure and steadfast, and which enters the Presence behind the veil.

Hebrews 6:19 (NKJV)

When we were growing up on boats at Lake Erie, anchors were a necessity. Anchors kept us securely positioned to fish hot spots. But an anchor proved most needed during unforeseen storms. As we fished miles out, unexpected storms could rapidly develop with 30–40 mph winds churning the lake into 8–10-foot waves. You couldn't outrun them; instead, you had to "batten down the hatches" and ride out the storm. To keep the boat from shifting sidelong by the wind and capsizing in the large waves, we'd anchor off the front bow. Long rope allowed the anchor's flukes to tip downward, securely gripping the mud and rock lake bottom. This tethering kept the bow pointed into the wind and the boat pivoted, preventing the crashing waves from hitting us broadside.

In sudden storms of life, we need an anchor for our souls. Storms of adversity descend, bringing the onslaught of crashing emotional waves. We feel we are going to capsize and drown. When facing the death of loved ones, and clouds of grief cast darkness over our coming days, we need survival hope—the reliability and character of a loving God confirming his Word as our sure anchor.

A few months ago, I experienced the need for a soul anchor. My only child—age 47 and perfectly fit, wife and mother of four children—suffered a stroke that damaged one-fourth of her right brain. Alone at home, she was not found for over eight hours. She arrived at the hospital with brain swelling, face drooping, and her left side limp and unresponsive.

A semi-conscious state with daily brain swelling were our threatening clouds. The prognosis wasn't good. "But she's young and fit so there is hope she will recover." The doctors reassured us, but the winds of adversity picked up momentum, threatening to capsize my faith and trust. Four daily brain scans showed continued swelling. Surgery was scheduled for day five to release the pressure. Our prayers seemed ineffective to calm our storm.

I needed Jesus to stop my storm. I needed my hope firm, fixed, and steadily directed into the wind, not broadsided with every new report. Getting alone in a hospital alcove, I opened my phone Bible app and scrolled to Psalm 34. I remembered it had verses about trusting God in a hard place. But my eyes hit the last verse of the previous Psalm. "Let your mercy, O Lord, be upon us, just as we hope in you" (Psalm 33:22 NKJV).

That's all the Holy Spirit needed. My anchor of hope dropped deeply into my soul, firm and resolute, bringing correction to my alignment with God. My volatile emotional course calmed. I was no longer tossed by crisis winds. I resolutely battened down the hatches, caught my breath, and knew change was coming. Fresh installments of faith, peace and hope displaced fear, anxiety, and hopelessness. Day five brought new reports. The brain swell had stopped. Hope had securely anchored, so mercy could bring our miracle.

Do you have an anchor in God ready for the sudden storms of life?

Jesus, help me to prepare for the sudden storms of life with my anchor in your Word and your character as a good God. Help me to firmly anchor my hopes in you my Rock so that I may weather life's chaotic storms. When waves crash over me, and darkness surrounds me, help me to keep my head above water. Jesus, speak peace to my storm.

“

....
....
....
....
....
....
....
....
....
....
....
....
....
....

The Bus Ministry

by Jeanne Roberson

Then the master said to the servant, "Go out into the highways and hedges, and compel them to come in, that my house may be filled.

Luke 14:23 (NKJV)

When I was eleven years old, my mother separated from my father for a while. As the only girl and the oldest, I was often responsible to help care for my younger siblings. During that time, a church group showed up at our door. They asked my father if we would like to attend their church. He declined to go, but agreed to allow me and my six brothers to attend because the church group offered to send a bus to pick us up and bring us home.

Every Sunday from then on, a big white school bus showed up at our house with the name Sunrise Boulevard Baptist Church painted on the side. The pastor, his wife, and the church congregation worked hard to teach us about Jesus during Sunday school, followed by the church service. We sang songs like "Jesus Loves Me," " Bringing in the Sheaves," and "The Old Rugged Cross."

We ranged in age from five to eleven and were an ornery

bunch to take on without parental supervision, but the church members all threw in a hand to make sure we behaved and listened. They took us to nursing homes to sing Christmas carols to the elderly and welcomed us at church picnics and special events. They disciplined us, when needed, and loved us unconditionally.

One Sunday, while Pastor Holtan gave the call to Christ, I accepted Jesus as my Savior and so did some of my brothers. We were baptized in a small pool behind the altar. Something in me changed after that. I had a sincere love for God and even though I couldn't see Him, I knew He was always with me. I prayed every day, and read my Bible. I wanted to be a good girl so I could please God.

Later, as a young adult, I walked away from God for many years. I returned to my faith while recovering from alcoholism. I went back to that little church, in hopes of finding those people who nurtured and led me to Christ. I wanted to thank them for what they did for me and share how my life turned out as an adult.

The pastor and his wife were still there. I had the opportunity to attend their Sunday service and share my testimony of how the bus ministry led me to my eternal salvation. Later, Pastor and Sister Holtan asked me to write an article for a Baptist newspaper sharing my story about the bus ministry and how it contributed to my salvation, which I did, and it was published.

I'm happy to add that these days I'm still singing Jesus loves me, only now I'm the one who's teaching it.

How far from your comfort zone will you travel to fill the house of the Lord?

Dear Heavenly Father, please equip us with words to compel and actions to motivate. We ask you to map our destinations, that we may fill the house of the Lord.

"

....
....
....
....
....
....
....
....
....
....
....
....
....
....

Do You Ever Lose Your Peace?

by Ruth Dyck

May God our Father and the Lord Jesus Christ give you grace and peace.

1 Corinthians 1:3 (NLT)

Salaam alekum means grace and peace. It is an Arabic greeting from South Sudan. Isn't grace and peace what we all desire?

My peace quickly faded a few months ago as I listened to my husband share in church our heading to South Sudan. We had been praying about leaving our home empty or trying to rent it out, but I did not think we had decided yet. He announced in church that as an answer to prayer, a Ukrainian couple would be living in our home while we were gone. My brain screamed, When was he going to talk to me about this? I knew there was talk of our community accepting Ukranian refugees, and it's not that he hadn't mentioned this as something to consider. Was this truly God's leading? I was coming home from Africa sooner than my husband to continue my Bible school studies in the Fall. The thought in my mind was, am I now pushed out of my own house so I can not come home on the weekends?

During a silent retreat two years earlier with my class at

Steinbach Bible College, while meditating on 1 Corinthians 13, verse 5 really spoke to me. "It (Love) does not demand its own way." At that retreat, I felt I heard the Holy Spirit whisper to me, "Ruth whenever you feel pushed, that isn't me." Giving in to feelings of being pushed to do something I really didn't want to do, or wasn't quite ready to do made me feel pushed out, overlooked, and not heard. Since then, I have also been learning to allow the Holy Spirit to enter those feelings and to ask myself, why am I feeling this way?

At times it is just a trigger of an old wound from which I need to receive healing and grace through forgiveness. At times it is an attack and spiritual warfare. The enemy knows my weaknesses and knows how to push my buttons, so to speak. There are times I need wisdom to not go where I am feeling pushed to go, and there are times when I am being challenged not to be so pushy. In every instance it is an opportunity to grow more self-aware and mature more in tune with the Holy Spirit.

In this particular instance, after my husband made the surprise announcement about what he saw as an answer to prayer, I took a step back. I was able to speak to my hubby, and we sincerely prayed together. God's grace and peace began filling my heart.

I was challenged by the Holy Spirit to walk in his love and not demand my own way, which would have been to leave our home empty. As we moved forward with our plans to go to South Sudan, not only did friends come and do extra painting and packing up of some of our things in preparation for the Ukranian couple, I also had multiple offers for places to stay when needed.

God's grace abundantly met our financial needs with the

rental income, and we have had someone to care for our home during our absence. Plus we were instrumental in meeting the couple's needs as well. My initial feelings of being pushed out have turned once again to incredible peace because of God's grace.

What is something in your life that causes you to lose your peace and how can you find restoration?

Father, would you make me aware of when feelings bubble up in me that threaten me losing my peace. Please pour out your grace on me in those times so your Holy Spirit can reveal what my feelings are saying. Reveal past hurts that need healing through forgiveness or when I need to battle the enemy. Thank you for transforming my selfish heart from demanding my own way to walking in love, grace and peace. Amen.

"

....
....
....
....
....
....
....
....
....
....
....
....
....
....

Made Worthy, Trust God

by Susanne Moore

Yea though I walk through the valley of the shadow of death, I will fear no evil: for thou art with me.

Psalm 23:4 (KJV)

When I was a young girl, God began planting his Word into my heart. I memorized scripture to win prizes. I competed in Bible bowls (competitions to look up Scriptures). I took notes during sermons and events. I went to church with a neighbor who was kind enough to ask. I even sang in an a capella quartet all through high school, while also living in the world.

God pursued me through heartbreaking tragedies, one right after the other: poverty, abuse, rape, alcoholics, more abusers, divorce, cancer. Must I go on? By the world's standards my life has been one of those memoirs that make you cringe until you reach the merciful, joy-filled pasture on the other side. The Lord was right there with me. God's Word was dug down deep into my soul and it saved my life over and over and over.

In the fourth grade, I memorized the entire twenty-third Psalm in the King James Version, for a chance to pull a prize out of a box. Little trinkets that made a sad little girl feel good. This one verse in particular rises from within every single time I walk through hard spaces because I have walked through the valley of the shadow of death. God was and is with me.

God sat beside me, waving his hands in front of my face, holding me, even in pain, even in shame, in all the seemingly impossible moments. He walked with me when I was afraid. He spoke to me through hymns and through others. He helped me through every single day. The toy was a 6" ruler, the prize was the planting—what an extraordinary way to measure God's faithfulness and my worth.

My value is not measured by what people might think of me or the 6-inch ruler of the world. You know the limited, weak, sadly cunning enemy will try to get to me in my vulnerability or my fears. He attempts to drag me down to that little girl who thought pleasing people made her valuable. For you this could be other situations like the loss of a job, or the hurt from someone in the church. Those are just unfortunate happenings in our daily act of living. They do not in any way measure the value of our soul.

My worth is found in the Lord. It is measured by an audacious God, who sent his son Jesus to save my life, created me in his image, numbered the hairs on my head (and freckles on my skin), and the weight on my bones. He gently spreads his words to the ends of the earth for me, for you. I was made worthy; you are made worthy.

Trusting God means we trust his Word. Believing God means we know that we are worth his tireless pursuit to restore, repair, rejuvenate and redeem our life. He loves me; he loves you. The past years are gone. God was there, in the middle of the mess, prompting us through tiny measures of mercy and grace to bring us to the brink of the world and nudging us to leap gloriously into our worthiness. Trust God that you are made worthy.

Heavenly Father, I praise you for I am fearfully and wonderfully made. I am so delighted in the life found on the other side of the pasture. Taking a leap into your arms has been the most rewarding, renewing, refreshing time. Thank you for loving me through the madness. I pray for the people reading these stories, that they can solidify their belief, remove the doubt, trust your pursuit, and truly find their worth in your arms. Thank you for making us worthy in you.

In Christ's name I pray, amen.

“

....
....
....
....
....
....
....
....
....
....
....
....
....
....

A Sin, a Cross, or a Thorn?

by Patricia Butler

I am the Lord, who heals you.

Exodus 15:26 (NIV)

If Jesus healed others, why not me? Do I lack faith? Is this a thorn on my side? My cross to bear?

These questions arose after an accident left me with severe spinal injuries and a "permanent" disability. In constant pain, I slid into depression, anger, and grief, but throughout my twelve-year journey, I never stopped badgering God for healing. God reveals himself as "Jehovah-Rapha, the Lord who heals you." I would hold him to it.

I held on with Job's tenacity. Friends showed up—as they did for Job—with speeches, advice, and beliefs that frustrated, angered, and confused me. *It's not God's will. Are you in sin? His grace is sufficient. You are healed—just claim it.*

People meant well or sincerely believed these statements (some of which are true). But their speeches, advice, and beliefs drove me (like Job) to declare my innocence and persist for Jehovah-Rapha's answer.

Returning to the Exodus story, I noticed more. The Israelites were crossing a desert and had been three days without water. When they found some, too bitter to drink, they complained. God instructed Moses to throw a stick in the water, and when he did, God healed the waters (Exodus 15:25). What instructions might he have for me?

Crossing my desert of pain, I had a bitter pill to swallow—the label, permanent disability. I complained but nothing changed. Maybe Jesus wouldn't heal me; he didn't heal everyone. But until he said no, I wouldn't quit. Like the persistent widow, I banged on heaven's door for justice.

My questions followed me to France, where I worked as a missionary and discovered demonic spirits in others. Seeking help, I studied Scripture, read books, and talked to pastors and other missionaries. Little did I know, God was setting the stage for my healing.

Twelve years after the accident, in my quest to understand demonic spirits, I stumbled into a healing conference, where God met me with his own questions. Midway through the week, he pinpointed a forgotten anger, buried in the pain.

"What did you do with that anger?" he whispered. "Don't let the sun set on your anger. Don't give the enemy a foothold" (Ephesians 4:26).

I gulped. Twelve years of sunsets had passed. That evening, God's next question came.

"Did you forgive the driver responsible for your accident?"

Two questions unraveled twelve years of pain and disability. With my confession, repentance, and forgiveness, Jehovah-Rapha healed bitter waters, recalibrated my spine, and pronounced, “Woman, you are set free from your infirmity” (Luke 13:12 NIV).

I entered the conference stiff and bent, with a tentative gait from the pain of several herniated discs in my neck. I left upright, pain-free, and energized. Two decades later, I remain free of back pain, spasms, and herniated discs. I resumed normal activities and one supernatural one: following the Healer, setting others free with questions and prayer.

If you or someone you love had an infirmity, what questions would you ask Jehovah-Rapha?

Lord, Jehovah-Rapha, may each one reading these words enjoy good health. May it go well with them, even as their soul gets along well. In Jesus' name, amen.

“

....
....
....
....
....
....
....
....
....
....
....
....
....
....

Reaping the Harvest

by Todd Ellis

For to everyone who has will more be given, and he will have an abundance.

Matthew 25:29 (ESV)

A quick tip for those of you who aren't farmers—it's a lot of work. It may look easy: planting a seed, letting God send his rain, and waiting. But, I assure you, there's a lot between sowing and reaping.

In Matthew 25:14-30, the parable of the talents, Jesus spoke of investing talents. A talent was a coin and came in a few varieties. The Hebrews and Romans both used them. Jesus told a story about a master who gave his servants talents and waited to see what they would do. The servants who invested them were rewarded with more talents. The one who didn't, well, let's just say the master wasn't too happy with him.

Back then, a talent was earned through labor just like today's currency. By using our gifts, or God-given talents, a person earned money. Much like today.

Today we can look at our talents as the gifts God has given us, to be developed for God's glory. In order to bring our talent to fruition, we must cultivate it by developing it to our utmost ability.

The difficulty comes through doubts and discouragement. But this is where it gets good! God loves to work through us like he did with David, the shepherd boy. The future king David stepped into his courageous destiny by using his talents, the skills he developed in the fields. God gave us talents for our destiny.

God knows our struggles and has already blessed our journey as the hero. Our talents, faithfully used, bring him glory.

When we courageously develop our talent into a skill, we are taking a leap of faith, trusting God at his Word. He loves this! The Bible shows over and over that this is pleasing to God.

When we sow our talents, and faithfully develop them into skills for God's glory, our steps become more clear. Clarity comes as we get closer to God. Doubt and fear dissolve and we can hear God's voice more clearly.

As we align to his purpose for us, by sowing our talents through faith, we plant seeds and trust God for the growth.

We reap the fruits of our labor by giving God the glory for our accomplishments. Faith like a farmer lets us obediently follow the call of God even during the seasons of waiting.

It's in the waiting, as the seed of faith is taking root, when God is doing his great work of faith. It's the same when we plant a seed in our garden. When the seed is deeply embedded in the soil, the transformation from seed to plant begins.

At first the seed hull is broken open and the roots, small at first, begin to grow. Notice which direction the roots grow, towards the sun. The DNA, implanted by our Creator, into the seed, gives them an internal direction, when followed.

Isn't that the same with us? When we follow the direction of the Holy Spirit we grow towards the Son, Jesus. When the invisible work of the Holy Spirit is being done, in the soil of our hearts, it seems like nothing is happening, like it's invisible even to the One above.

But, that is where the greatest work of seed faith is being done. By staying faithful in the invisible world of faith, we please God and move closer to His true purposes in our lives.

When have you reaped a bountiful harvest by developing your talent and taking a leap of faith?

God let me faithfully plant the seeds of faith and patiently wait for the harvest.

"

....
....
....
....
....
....
....
....
....
....
....
....
....
....

Wallflower to God's Chosen

by Nancy O'Meara

But you are a chosen people, a royal priesthood, a holy nation, God's special possession, that you may declare the praises of him who called you out of darkness into his wonderful light.

1 Peter 2:9 (NIV)

I remember as a child many times being overlooked or chosen last on the playground for the dodgeball team, basketball team, etc. You know the feeling when there are two or three left, and you just pray you will not be chosen last? Or how about the eighth-grade party when you were never asked to dance? Never quite made it to the "cool kids" group. I was a wallflower until I met Jesus. Have you ever felt imperfect, unequipped to inspire others?

What if we look at all of this in a different way? Have you ever thought your imperfections would inspire others to overcome adversity?

I have had many years to ponder this question and have come to this conclusion. God chose imperfect people to fulfill his purpose throughout the Bible and he does the same today. We are all imperfect but we are his chosen people, God's special possession, created to declare his praises. He took us out of darkness into his light because of his great love for us.

Peter, a disciple of Jesus, is a splendid example of how God used an imperfect man. Even after Peter denied he knew Jesus three times, Jesus still used imperfect Peter to minister to crowds of people, sharing the gospel. Jesus told Peter "And I tell you that you are Peter and, on this rock, I will build my church.

Moses felt inadequate to speak to the Israelites on behalf of God. He told God, "I have never been eloquent, neither in the past nor since you have spoken to your servant. I am slow of speech and tongue." But God chose Moses and helped him speak and told him what to say. God went on to give Moses complete directions and used Moses' imperfections to lead the Israelites out of Egypt. He always equips us in order for His will to be done.

The I AM WHO I AM gives us new life through our faith and trust in his Son, who died in our place on the cross, so that we can be forgiven and spend eternity with him.

He loves us with an everlasting love. Because of this love and grace, we can put our faith in Jesus for forgiveness and eternal life. He called us out of darkness into the light that illuminates his love.

We no longer must live as a wallflower in fear of not being significant enough or perfect enough to be God's special possession.

Let us celebrate as we light up the world with his love.

How will you use your imperfections as God's Chosen to help others find their way out of darkness into the light of God's Love?

Dear Jesus, thank you for choosing me and bringing me out of darkness into your glorious light. Thank you for providing me with the tools to use my imperfections to share the love of the gospel with others. Please guide me to those who need you and give me the courage to step out in your love with the hope that others will find forgiveness and eternal life with you. Amen.

"

....

....

....

....

....

....

....

....

....

....

....

....

....

....

Lifting All the Weights

by Teresa Janzen

And there are also many other things that Jesus did, which if they were written one by one, I suppose that even the world itself could not contain the books that would be written.
John 21:25 (NKJV)

My coworker is an avid fitness buff who likes to go to the gym after work. Her departing phrase is often, "Today I'm going to lift all the weights." This means she has a serious workout in mind, and she is excited about it. It's a big plan—not just to lift the small, easy weights, nor only the big, impressive ones. By lifting all the weights, she builds both strength and endurance.

For me, the idea of lifting all the weights at a gym would be equivalent to torture. While I'm not a bodybuilder, I do understand my coworker's enthusiasm. As a writer, it's how I feel when I use words to describe what God has done in my life.

My idea of a spiritual workout would be to sit at my desk and write all the words that praise and glorify God. Not just the easy words of praise that come when life goes my way, but also the groans of surrender that come when my heart is heavy.

John acknowledges his writing is only a small account of

Jesus' works. Many other things that Jesus did, as well as signs he gave his disciples after his resurrection, went unrecorded. John chose the words he wrote so his readers might believe Jesus was the Christ, the Son of God, and that they might have life in his name. Just imagine if we could read all the words that describe the amazing things Christ did during his earthly ministry.

Meditating on what God has done is a great spiritual workout and builds faith muscles. Sharing those things with others is an even more extreme workout. Our testimony invites others to see, believe, and experience God's goodness for themselves. When we fill our minds with what God has done for us, we will be ready and eager to share our story.

One of my favorite hymns is, The Love of God is Greater Far by Frederick M. Lehman (1917). The third stanza states,

Could we with ink the ocean fill,
and were the skies of parchment made;
were ev'ry stalk on earth a quill,
and ev'ryone a scribe by trade;
to write the love of God above
would drain the ocean dry;
nor could the scroll contain the whole,
though stretched from sky to sky.

Think about the small, everyday ways God is present in your life. What are some words you can use to describe his everyday presence? Now think of when God has intervened in your big moments. Try to use some unique words to explain to someone else what God's provision means to you.

Loving Father, your grace and mercy are too great to describe. In fact, there are many ways you care for me that I may not even know about. Thank you for your everyday provision as well as your extraordinary intervention. Help me to see you in the large and small moments of this day. Amen.

"

....

....

....

....

....

....

....

....

....

....

....

....

....

....

God's Faithfulness throughout the Generations

A Wild Kind of Legacy

by Teresa Janzen

Now to him who is able to do far more abundantly than all that we ask or think, according to the power at work within us, to him be glory in the church and in Christ Jesus throughout all generations, forever and ever. Amen.

Ephesians 3:20-21 (ESV)

My grandmother was born on the prairies of Iowa as the family moved west to seek their fortune. A few years later, my Great Grandfather abandoned his wife and three children in a wild west town in Texas while he returned to a more civilized existence in Michigan. Great Grandma Eva survived by marrying John, a kind, yet stern man willing to take on another man's responsibilities.

It seems like a chapter out of a western romance novel, but it's my family history. Those experiences, and the choices made by each person involved, shaped my grandmother into the woman she came to be. She then nurtured my mom, the best she knew how, and then my mom reared me.

When I think about the individuals who came before me, I have a sense of gratitude and wonder. We don't have anyone extraordinary in the family that I know of. Just normal people making mistakes, learning lessons, and trying to get along. We were generally blue-collar workers; my mom was the first in the family to go to college. Faith wasn't even a big part of our tradition. In later years, my grandmother watched television evangelists as her only church activity.

Yet somehow it has all come around to me in my generation. How is it that I came to know and love the Lord? My story is as individual as yours, but we share one thing in common—Jesus. Nothing I have done, nor anything you have done, has resulted in salvation. We can't rest on our family laurels, if indeed there were any. It is Christ, and Christ alone, who saves.

Even Jesus has a few crooked branches in his family tree, yet it is through him that families are healed and generational curses are smashed. No matter how unlikely each individual in Christ's genealogy seemed to be during his or her time in history, their lineage led exactly where God intended.

Families come in all kinds and configurations. Some look spiffy on the outside, but they may be just as broken as mine on the inside. I don't know how long my great grandmother was on her own with her children in that wild west town. I wonder if she prayed, and I wonder if she saw John as an answer to her prayer. The only answer for hurting people in broken families is Christ, yet God chooses to use people to accomplish his work and share the hope of Christ.

God remains faithful throughout the generations. Your family tree may have broken and severed branches like mine. Maybe you even have some wilted twigs and a few grafted sprouts. Whether your loved ones are walking with the Lord at present or wandering in the desert, God is faithful.

His plan is one of restoration and hope. He doesn't leave his children abandoned, but he also doesn't make them stay when they choose to run away. Rather he waits patiently, sending unlikely people to pick up the pieces in unexpected ways.

Are there parts of your family tree that need the healing touch of the master gardener today?

Father God, thank you for being faithful to my family through the years, even when we were not faithful to you. As you have so often healed my broken heart and restored my wounded spirit, I pray for my loved ones who have wandered far from you. Bring the right people into their life to be the instrument of your rescue and hope. Amen.

"

....
....
....
....
....
....
....
....
....
....
....
....
....
....

Grandma's Lap

by Linda Summerford

When I am afraid, I put my trust in you

Psalm 56:3 (NIV)

Lightning pierced the sky like a knife on fire. Thunder rolled around the house until it shook. Tears ran down my cheeks as I called out to Grandma. My little sister and I ran to Grandma's lap. She rocked us back and forth as she softly sang to us and whispered Scripture verses in our ears.

"When I am afraid, I will put my trust in you," she would quote from Scripture. "Don't be afraid, girls. God is just watering all the beautiful trees and flowers. Let's sing praises to him and thank him."

Then, as she sang "Jesus Loves Me," the fear melted away. No one calmed our fears like Grandma.

In 1956, the authorities pulled my sister and me out of an abusive home. We dealt with extreme anxiety and abandonment and many other things we didn't understand. By the time we were three and five years old, we had a new family and the memories of our older sister and brother were beginning to fade.

I have no doubt God hand-selected our new family, complete with this wonderful Grandma who would introduce me to him. It would have been easy for me to feel unlovable. I already believed someone didn't love me enough to keep me.

God calmed my fears through my Grandma's care. She offered me unconditional love, and when I looked deep into her eyes I knew I belonged. Her face glowed with excitement every time she saw me come into a room. Through her love, I learned that God is sovereign and had a better plan for my life. He wanted me to find her. Grandma's unconditional love and forgiveness taught me how to love and forgive others. Grandma's love became real for me because I experienced it through her acceptance.

Being confined to her wheelchair from arthritis never diminished her love. In her earlier years, Grandma was the pianist in her church. As time passed, arthritis twisted her hands, but she could still play the piano and sing so beautifully that it brought tears to my eyes. I never witnessed any bitterness from her. Maybe that's why I've never felt resentment for what happened to me. She impressed upon me to never carry anger in my heart, as it would only cause pain.

Grandma also taught me to let go of circumstances I cannot control. Grandma's quiet, sweet spirit spoke volumes to my heart. She never shouted. She never preached. She just lived out her love for God before me and I learned by her example that I could trust him.

I still catch myself at times beginning to panic when storms come into my life. My insecurities can still haunt me. But then I remember what Grandma told me so many times when I came to her with a problem. The wisdom and insight I learned while sitting in Grandma's lap carried me through my teen years and into adulthood. It's one I now pass on to my grandchildren with the hope that it will help guide generations to come.

What memories are you planting in your children and grandchildren's hearts that will stay with them throughout their lives?

Lord, when situations arise that I cannot control, and I am fearful, remind me to put my trust in you. You are all powerful, all knowing, and the only one who is in control of all. Help me to remember that, and to turn to you for comfort and peace. In Jesus' name, amen.

"

....
....
....
....
....
....
....
....
....
....
....
....
....
....

By His Grace

by Leann Seale

All the ways of the Lord are loving and faithful.

Psalm 25:10 (NIV)

The Lord overwhelmed me with his faithfulness and mercy, tenderly caring for my fragile heart. A huge change was taking place in the life of our family, and I am not a fan of change. Our oldest of four sons would be moving out and heading to Azusa Pacific University. Although he would not be far away, life as we knew it would be changing forever. I've dreaded this season for years, I believe since kindergarten! Although I was excited for my son and all that he would experience, the thought of his empty chair at our dinner table was more than I could take, and my heart was breaking.

By God's grace, the transition was gradual. Because my son moved into his dorm room well before the actual "move-in day," there was plenty of back and forth from dorm to home, and even a dinner or two with the family.

Once orientation was complete and official send-offs were over, our life was also in full swing. Our other boys were busy with school sports and church activities, my husband was working more than usual, and I was planning for fall ministries. Our dinner table was made up of whoever was home at the time, and not once was everyone home for dinner—until three weeks later. I had to check the calendar because this was so out of the norm. You see, dinner in our house is the time when we come together to pray, reconnect, share thoughts and ideas, teach our kids, and listen to one another's "good and bad thing" for the day.

On this evening, I was preparing a big dinner, where we'd all eat together. My mind was on planning to help lead a Bible study, which would begin the following morning. I was giving the devotion, so my mind was filled with what I'd be sharing, as well as with the preparation of prayer cards and goody bags for my small group. As we sat down to dinner, the chair across from where my husband sits was empty, yet dinner conversation was lively and upbeat.

It wasn't until dinner was over and my husband and I were left at the table that I realized what God had done for me. Through tears, I told my husband that God had carried me through those three weeks, filling my time, heart, and soul with the ministry I loved. By his grace, I did not crumble. He filled my heart with a new intensity for the ministries I was involved in, and he lovingly gave me weeks before only the five of us would sit around that table. I know friends and family were praying for me during this time, and I felt carried.

God is always faithful, and he overwhelms me with his compassion. His love is beautifully evident, especially through difficult seasons. It is during those times that I find the Psalms help express what is on my heart and remind me of God's character.

Are you going through a season of change and need a reminder of God's faithfulness? Consider reading the Psalms, letting them permeate your heart and refresh your soul.

Dear Heavenly Father, you are gracious, loving, and faithful. I am grateful that when I go through difficult seasons, you are there right alongside me, allowing me to tangibly feel your love and care. You overwhelm me with your compassion. Praise you and thank you. In Jesus' name, Amen.

“

....
....
....
....
....
....
....
....
....
....
....
....
....
....

Far From the Tree

by Teresa Janzen

...these I will bring to my holy mountain
and give them joy in my house of prayer.
Their burnt offerings and sacrifices
will be accepted on my altar;
for my house will be called
a house of prayer for all nations.
Isaiah 56:7 (NIV)

My daughter was surprised by the question, "Is your mother's name Teresa?"

My oldest daughter was 13 when we returned to the small town where I had lived growing up. We resembled one another so much that she learned to expect the question of her parentage in church and social gatherings. While physical resemblance is common from one generation to the next, personalities and behavior can vary.

Sometimes I like to hear my adult children use the same words I said to them when they were small, but other times I cringe when they display some of my attributes. We want to leave a positive legacy. How a child is raised will contribute to the adult they become, but we must remember that they are their own person – for good or bad, failures and successes. We don't get to hand-pick the attributes they acquire.

In spite of his numerous and grievous faults, King David was known as a man after God's own heart. Still God didn't allow David to fulfil his dream of building a temple for the Lord because he was also a man of war, and God ordained the temple to be a house of prayer for all nations . God gifted Solomon a reign during a time of peace and enabled him to fulfill his father's vision to build the temple. But even Solomon made plenty of mistakes of his own during his reign.

It feels great when our children experience success, but we should be careful to not rob them of the joy of their accomplishment by trying to take credit. Solomon brought honor to his father by building the temple, but he also acknowledged the temple was built to honor his father's (Solomon's) God—who had brought about the circumstances to allow the temple to be built.

Conversely, when an adult child behaves in a way contrary to what we would hope for them, we need to identify the extent and limitation of our role in the situation. We may advise, support, apologize if wrong, encourage, empathize, grieve, and pray; but we cannot control or mitigate the outcome or consequences of their choices. Nor should we accept guilt beyond any actual involvement we may have had in the incident.

We want our children to pick up our good traits and improve on our faults, but the reality is they are their own unique person and are influenced by a combination of many factors. If we wounded a child at some point in their upbringing, it is important to apologize and seek reconciliation if it is in their best interest now. If a child succeeds, celebrate with them without claiming their victory.

Am I unfairly claiming honor or carrying shame for choices and circumstances made by the adult children I've cared for?

Father God, thank you for the children you have placed in my care. Help me to guide and influence them through various stages of life with your wisdom and point the glory to you.

"

....

....

....

....

....

....

....

....

....

....

....

....

....

....

Wheels of Faith

by Susanne Moore

He provides food for those who fear him; he remembers his covenant forever.

Psalm 111:5 (ESV)

Has God ever given you something that was just amazing? I remember when God gave me a car. My previous car had blown an engine, and I was broke. In fact, through the years, God gave my daughters and I five cars. Not just old clunkers either—Chrysler New Yorker, Cadillac Deville, Nissan Maxima, Toyota Camry, and a full conversion van with internal running lights. Oh, how my kids still miss that van. They bring it up often because we did some crazy, fun things in that van with friends, soccer teams, choir kids, and family.

I have been a single mother since one daughter was in diapers and the other was three. Now they are both married with their own families and careers. However, the testimony of God's commitment to be faithful has never wavered.

God bestowed his gifts of grace on us three girls in countless, unimaginable, only possible-through-him ways, from

$5 refund checks that put bread on the table to big things, such as vehicles and a $2500 check from a stranger. Of course, it is not just about finances; that just happens to be where I have struggled. Isn't it cool that he built trust in me exactly where I failed?

I get excited when someone asks me, "How do you know God is faithful?" I love sharing about God's steadfast loyalty. Many people find it hard to believe in the invisible. Obviously, a car or a refund check are tangible. You can feel, touch, taste, see, or smell it. What are the odds it would arrive exactly when your check ran out and you needed something to make the week? Who prompted the giver?

Faith is believing that God is working in and through the everyday humdrum of living. It is trusting that he gave us life, he has a purpose, he knows our needs, and he is working all the time. God's work becomes clear when you are struggling with self-worth and a random elderly man tells you how beautiful you look today. Or when you are late for work and you drive past a ten-car pile-up that happened when you were originally supposed to be passing by.

I do not believe in chance or luck. God is in control of everything—the unspoken, hidden, in between, under, inside, outside, upside, downside. He is the beginning and the end. God is there, faithfully fulfilling his covenant with his children to the very end.

He loves us unconditionally, no matter how much we falter in trusting him. Guess what? God is still and without exception delivering on his promises, for he is never failing and forever trustworthy. God hears and is working for you and through you.

How can you personally give account of God's dedication, devotion, and dependability to you, so you can build up the faith in God for those around you?

Heavenly Father, how much I treasure the memories of all you have provided me and my family. Remembering these things helps build up our commitment to continue trusting you in our everyday life. I pray that every story and every word is received with that plucking of the heart strings, flooding our memories of days of your faithfulness. Remind us that you hear us, that we can believe in your promises, that you are deep in the trenches with us, and that you are leading us out. Build us up, refine our souls, and bring us home one moment at a time. Thank you for giving us life and purpose, knowing our needs, and intimately loving us right where we struggle.

In Jesus' name I pray, amen.

"

....
....
....
....
....
....
....
....
....
....
....
....
....
....

Daddy's Hands

by Susanne Moore

But now, O Lord, you are our Father; we are the clay, and you are our potter; we are all the work of your hand.

Isaiah 64:8 (ESV)

It was after midnight and I was dead asleep when the phone rang. Hanging up, I threw on a pair of shorts and a t-shirt and rushed out. The wind blew softly as I jumped into my little white 84 Chevy Chevette (not Corvette). Turning the key, I sighed loudly as the realization hit me hard and a heaviness settled in my chest. I was tired of calls like this.

Driving at a mad pace, I suddenly had to slam on my brakes to turn into the Burger King parking lot. I could see the police car's flashing lights and intentionally drove past to peruse the situation myself.

Mom's white Ford Ranger was haphazardly stopped in the circular part of the drive thru. The passenger front tire was up on the curb. I pulled into a parking space and walked over.

"Hello, Officer. I am his sister. Thank you for not taking him in." My little brother was sitting in the driver seat with his head slumped over.

The policeman spoke with a kindness that made me pause. “I was young once. I see he has already been in trouble. Let’s get him into your car, and then you can help me push the truck out of the way.”

My brother had been drinking and apparently was pulling in to buy himself something to eat. My mother’s truck already had a breathalyzer installed months before for her indiscretions. It is possible that he couldn’t restart the truck when the machine ordered him to breathe to reset. I did not have all the details; however, I knew God was there, folding grace into my brother’s soul.

As I look back on days like this, remembering one of countless tragic realities we faced in our youth, I see a path that led each of us straight to Jesus. Do policemen make calls like this? I believe it is an impossibility without God whispering a merciful prompt into the heart of that man.

God intervened in my brother’s life and mine that day and innumerable other days. Although many other things had to happen, just like Jesus had to suffer and take on our sin so that we too might have everlasting life, each moment of redirection turned our hearts towards acceptance of Jesus as our Savior. Like clay on a pottery wheel, my Daddy’s heavenly hands worked on each of us, refining, changing and shaping our lives—a beautiful undoing of generational sin and transformational grace. Life can be tragic, but the Lord is a masterful potter, and he does not stop working until he takes us home to him.

Seeing Jesus in your narrative, even when it is devastating, helps you see the small, intricate details of a God who truly does direct your steps even before you or your family or your friends know him.

Do you see God's interventions in your narrative drawing you closer to Jesus?

Heavenly Father, thank you for the testimony of your footprints of grace in the twists and turns of our lives. I pray that everyone who reads this has glimpses of you as they take time to consider how they arrived at this exact moment in their walk towards you and with you. Open the eyes of our hearts to see you taking this piece of modern clay and shaping us into your glorious image by the works of your almighty hands. We thank you and praise you for intervening in our lives and bringing us home.

“

....
....
....
....
....
....
....
....
....
....
....
....
....
....

This Time Next Year

by Maureen Miller

Is anything too hard for the Lord? At the appointed time I will return to you, about this time next year, and Sarah shall have a son.

Genesis 18:14 (ESV)

By this time next year? That's what God said in May 1996. For several years, I'd been hearing from him—through rainbow sightings and, strange as it sounds, 5:12s.

It began one morning several years earlier. In a dream-state, I saw a rainbow and asked the Lord, "What does it mean?"

"A promise will be fulfilled."

I knew—the promise to give us a child. Doctors had deemed me infertile. "Void a miracle, you'll never have biological children." Still, despite those words, I'd learned to pray with palms up and open, giving my dreams to God that he might fill me with his desires for me. Psalm 37:4 spoke particularly to this, reminding me that, as I delighted in the Lord, he'd deposit his dream seeds in my soul.

On that rainbow morning, I awoke and knew. God was

saying yes to my desire. My part was to pray to that end, even if it meant waiting, even if things happened differently than I imagined.

After that rainbow dream, I'd see God's bow in the sky and praise him for his promise fulfilled, even though I wasn't yet a mom. And then he began using 5:12s as further confirmation.

I'd wake up at exactly 5:12 or see billboards or marquees with 5:12 in bold font. I'd receive mail with 5/12 at the top and see these numbers on the television screen. God is creative. I imagine he smiled as I chronicled his faithfulness in my journal over the years.

Then, on that late May morning when, in my quiet time, he led me to Genesis 18, my heart danced. Abraham and Sarah, encountering three visitors, are told that Sarah will have a son when visited the following year. I wondered if God meant I'd get pregnant and have a baby a year from then, or, perhaps, I'd discover on that specific date I was expecting.

I asked him, "What's this about?"

He answered with a question. "What was Mother's Day this year, just weeks ago?"

I knew. "May 12."

"Indeed. Next May 12, you will have a son."

Faithful to his word, the following May 12, I did have a son, though my husband and I wouldn't know it for nine months.

Our firstborn was carried in the womb of a woman not yet twenty. Despite her love for her unborn child, she wasn't prepared to parent. Thus, she chose to place him for adoption.

It wasn't until after his birth that she confided in me. "Ian was conceived on May 12, the night of my senior prom." Through tears, she continued, "His father was my boyfriend, though my parents didn't approve."

God fulfilled my desire when Cindy gave us her son. It came exactly when God said, according to his good and perfect plan. He prepared a way to bring our child home to our waiting arms.

What desires do you need to lift to the Lord, with palms up and open, that he might place his perfect plans in your surrendered heart?

Kind Father, thank you for your Word and all the ways you speak through it. Help me delight in you more by reading it and spending time with you in prayer, that you might fill me with all that's part of your perfect plan for my life. Amen.

"

Letting Go

by Teresa Janzen

My lord the king, the eyes of all Israel are on you, to learn from you who will sit on the throne of my lord the king after him

1 Kings 1:20 (NIV)

A slight jerk of the steering wheel and the car swerved away from the median barrier, but the young driver startled at the sudden movement and jerked the wheel back in the opposite direction. One overcorrection after another and the car was spinning out-of-control across four lanes of busy freeway.

It was the first time I'd let my daughter drive with other passengers in the car. What took mere seconds to transpire seemed to happen in slow motion. First one vehicle swerved around us on the right, then a semi-truck sped past on the left—air horn blaring. I glanced at my granddaughter peacefully buckled into the backseat. Is this the end of her short life? My body strained against the seatbelt as my head whipped forward with the impact into the guardrail on the opposite side of the road.

Teaching a young person to drive is a big responsibility. It can be dangerous, frightening, stressful—maybe even filled with tears or arguments. While an accident can occur during the learning process, it is almost certain to occur if the teacher grabs a hold of the steering wheel at every sign of trouble. Learners must be given the opportunity to manage challenges, experience success—and sometimes allowed to crash.

King David was nearing the end of his reign and life. He had told Bathsheba that God appointed their son Solomon as the next king of Israel, but he delayed turning loose of the kingdom. When Adonijah, David's son with Haggith, saw that his father wasn't transitioning power to the next generation, he took the initiative to raise supporters and declare himself king. David's reluctance to turn loose nearly ended with the wrong king on the throne .

David was comfortable in the driver's seat. While he had planned to turn over control of the kingdom to Solomon, he had failed to act on that plan. The people floundered without a strong leader. People feared for the future of the kingdom to the extent that when Adonijah put himself forward as successor there were plenty ready to support him.

Preparing children for leadership begins when they are young and are given household responsibilities. As young adults, they learn to manage their own schedules, finances, decisions, and motivations. There is a time when a parent may need to jump in and grab the wheel to prevent disaster, but as our children mature, we need to move to the passenger seat and let them maneuver the challenges. Eventually they go solo and our role shifts to that of a guide. Even then, our guidance can only be offered—not forced. Navigating these transitions takes courage and faith. It can be hard to know when to intervene and when to let them wobble for a while.

Am I jumping in to help at the first sign of trouble?

Lord, sometimes it's hard to know when to help and when to let go. Give me wisdom to know the difference. Help me to surrender those I love to your care at the right time. Amen.

"

....
....
....
....
....
....
....
....
....
....
....
....
....
....

The Journal

by Stacy Leicht

Delight yourself in the Lord, and he will give you the desires of your heart. Commit your way to the Lord, trust in him, and he will act. He will bring forth your righteousness as the light, and your justice as the noonday.

Psalm 37:4-6 (ESV)

I sat in a "Bride" bathrobe and fuzzy slippers. Mama served me heart-shaped pancakes smelling of sweet syrup. I did not have the guts to tell her I was not hungry. I cut a bite off the corner of the first pancake, knowing I'd never get it down. Mama hummed in the background, and her little feet pranced as she danced.

I was thrilled to be marrying the man of my dreams, but on my wedding day, reality began to sink in. This Is It! There would be no more humming in the background as someone else makes me breakfast. It was time to grow up and be a wife. It was going to be my turn to make the pancakes. Truth be told, I wasn't sure I even knew how to make pancakes.

My dad came in and softly touched the top of my head with his lips. "Look," He said. I recognized the black leather journal. I'd never looked in it, though it had been on his bedside table for years. It seemed private. He put the old leather journal down next to me. I hadn't realized it was so old and tattered. The pages were yellowed and stained, probably his morning black coffee. How long had he had this book?

Dad opened the book. I recognized his handwriting. He read the first entry, "Today, May 14, 1966. We had a daughter. We named her Stacy." He looked up and smiled at me with tears in his eyes.

"This book is a Prayer Journal. You can see the prayers your mother and I had for you throughout the pages. Some things were not always answered quickly, but God was always faithful to us."

He slid the book into my hands. Its soft black leather was warm from his touch. I saw the many prayers my parents raised on my behalf, including when I stepped in hot tar at the age of seven and had months of recovery.

I didn't have words, but tears began to flow. How could I possibly pack a bag today and leave this place called home? But then my father showed me the final entries—details of my relationship with my fiancé. They had prayed for me to meet and marry a Christian man, not just when I was of dating age, but from the time I was in diapers. "Dear Lord, we give Stacy to you, and know her life is in your hands. Please provide the perfect Christian man who will bring her closer to you."

I realized that my parents were a living testimony of Psalm 37:4-6. I hugged my father and mother. A great sense of peace overcame me. I was ready. It was all in the plan. God had ordained this day.

How can you provide generational love for your family, friends, and people you love in your life?

Dear Lord, help me to trust you. You say, "Do not be anxious about anything, but in everything by prayer and supplication with thanksgiving, let your requests be made known to God" (Proverbs 3:5). Help me stand firm and trust you completely. I desire to be dependent on you for all things. Amen.

"

....
....
....
....
....
....
....
....
....
....
....
....
....
....

Unimagined Wonder

by Nancy Kelley Alvarez

He does great things too marvelous to understand. He performs countless miracles.

Job 5:9 (NLT)

In high school I became a statistic: an unwed pregnant teenager. Reluctantly, with dread and despair, I concluded that adoption made the best sense. No other viable option presented itself.

At eighteen years old, my heart frozen in grief, I whispered goodbye to my little boy in the hospital nursery. The following months blurred. How I longed to hold him, smell his hair, and feel his baby skin. How was he impacted by our separation?

I finished college and moved to Asia to share Christ's love and truth. When my hope for love nearly drained away, Luke, a fellow missionary, dashed into my life. We married and I anticipated starting a family. When the fertility specialist said, "You should consider adoption," I wept at the irony.

For countless years, I searched the internet for my son, yearning to know if he thrived or barely coped. When I discovered his records could be opened, I prayerfully and fearfully submitted the paperwork. Within a matter of days, I received the call that my son wanted to connect with me!

Like a tilt-a-whirl, my emotions swooped between joy and fear. Would he be resentful? We scheduled our first talk. In a dreamlike state, I talked with Isaac for the very first time. He was now thirty-two and thankful for his loving adoptive parents.

I fell in love with this charming, compassionate, and gifted man who looked so much like me. He touched me deeply when he gave me a book of his baby pictures. A priceless treasure.

One day, I blurted out, "Would you like me to find your birth father?" Could I handle that?

"Yes, I would," he replied.

The Lord bolstered my courage as I contacted Jeremy. He immediately apologized and told me how God had transformed his life. The chains of resentment fell off and lightness filled me. He and his family eagerly welcomed Isaac.

My faith was tested, yet again, when Jeremy invited Luke and I to present our ministry to their home Bible study and spend the night at their home. Nerves and adrenaline rattled me. Could I face this family? When the day arrived, God's grace carried me through. And to my amazement, Jeremy's wife and I began a friendship. Over the years, all of us have grown close to Isaac.

Isaac even invited Luke and I to share a short presentation of our ministry at his church. Jeremy and his family came, and so did Isaac's adoptive father. When Isaac's father saw me chatting with Jeremy, he couldn't believe it. "She can stand to be in the same room with him?" Only God could do what seems impossible in such a breathtaking way.

In what way do you want God to work wondrously in your life and what steps of faith will you take?

Lord Jesus, I want to be filled with wonder at your mighty works. Help me to have faith and courage to do what you ask of me in order for that to happen. Forgive me when I hold resentment in my heart. Open my eyes to see the path you have for me. Give me the strength to take the first steps in the right direction.

“

....
....
....
....
....
....
....
....
....
....
....
....
....
....

Entrusting God with Life

by Chaplain Lisa Northway, U.S. Army

That is why I am suffering here in prison. But I am not ashamed of it, for I know the one in whom I trust, and I am sure that he is able to guard what I have entrusted to him until the day of his return.

2 Timothy 1:12 (NLT)

My husband and I boarded a plane for a military ministry conference in Washington, D.C. Before take-off, I received a text from my niece stating she received a message from someone looking for their birth mother.

This person believed their birthmother was her aunt and requested to make contact. Recalling a story I shared with her years ago, she realized this person might have a legitimate request. I suddenly remembered a message I received the evening before by a person with the same name. I returned to that message and discovered multiple messages containing information only the son I became pregnant with at the age of seventeen could know. Not trusting my voice to mouth words properly in the moment, I silently shared these messages with my husband to explain that this was my firstborn child I had lovingly entrusted to God and two Christian parents-to-be.

It had been over four decades since I held my baby boy. After being sent away to a home for unwed mothers, the time came to say goodbye to him. I remembered the day I prayed over him through tear-filled eyes. I knew it was the hardest and most selfless decision I would ever make as a teenager, and quite possibly in my entire life. I also knew enough about God that I could entrust him with this decision because he loved me and my child more than I could fully comprehend.

In the years following, I was also glad I took a vow not to pass on family secrets. I knew of their damage in multi-generations of my family. That commitment of continued trust in God bore fruit as my second-born adult child encouraged me to improve the possibility he could meet his only sibling. I submitted my DNA for the possibility of being found by my child if he chose, at some point, to pursue meeting members of his birth family. I never believed God owed me or promised me I would have the privilege of seeing my first-born child again this side of eternity. In addition, I do have a firmly held belief that God knows our deepest desires and hopes of those people we choose to ultimately place in his loving and trustworthy arms.

A few weeks later my husband boarded another flight to the West Coast. Soon we were both getting to know a man who was well loved by his adoptive parents, though he had also suffered a deep loss. We've also known the joy of adding a daughter-in-law and grandson to our family.

As our story unfolds, with complications common to many families, we have no doubt this was the best time to be revealed and be acquainted with each other. We know there will be growing pains ahead. We also know we serve a God we can trust with the hard things of life. We serve a God who gave us more than we knew to ask for this side of eternity! Our God is faithful and will not withhold good from us as we give him glory for the ministry of reconciliation he provides in our lifetime.

What hard choice have you entrusted to God? Do you desire to trust God in a greater way? Ask the Holy Spirit to help you commit that situation to him today.

Dear Heavenly Father, you know my thoughts and concerns. Please reveal to me anything I still need to trust you with regarding my past, present or future. May the enemy of my soul be kept from weaponizing my situation to shame me. I choose to trust you to reveal and reconcile situations for my good and your glory over my lifetime.

"

....
....
....
....
....
....
....
....
....
....
....
....
....
....

A Heavenly Lens

by Cherie Denna

He has made everything beautiful in its time. Also He has put eternity in their hearts, except that no one can find out the work that God does from beginning to end.

Ecclesiastes 3:11 (NKJV)

Several people closest to me are in the middle of life storms. A friend just lost her husband due to a sudden illness. A family member is suffering with the progression of dementia. Another's life uprooted after walking away from a toxic relationship, which spanned more than half her years. Emotions run high and hearts are shattered.

According to tradition, King Solomon authored the Book of Ecclesiastes in his old age. As he reflects on his life, Solomon refers to even the most painful life seasons as beautiful and appropriate. Life's most beautiful moments usually include weddings, babies, and autumn colors. Certainly, there is nothing beautiful about a time to weep or mourn (3:4), or a time to hate or make war (3:8), right?

It is possible to view our painful seasons through a heavenly lens. You may ask, "But, how can I possibly see anything beautiful or appropriate in this when my whole world has rocked off its foundation?"

I understand. It is a valid question. The truth: God is omnipotent. He has unlimited power and authority over every circumstance, as written in Ephesians 1:18-21. If we keep our eyes on him and seek him in the depth of our struggles and suffering, we get to witness these Scriptures come to life.

Our family can testify to this as we walk alongside my father-in-love through this season with dementia. His thoughts are often in a frenzy. No matter how prepared we thought we were, everyone is impacted. Overcome with an urgency to "do something," Pops began praying more each day for family and friends. Anyone, really. In just one month, he has led many of them to salvation in Jesus Christ. Regardless of the frustrations, Pops says he has never felt so much joy. He told the family, "It's beautiful, but I wish I would have started these conversations years ago. I have wasted so much time." I reminded him that everything is made beautiful in its time, not ours. The urgency Pops experiences is God's anointing on him. He reads more Scripture everyday which is the healthiest thing for him. His list of names helps him keep track of hearts who he must share the good news with. The Lord has given him divine purpose, just as promised.

Whether it is time to mourn or time to give up, God wastes no time when it comes to calling his children. His plan and purpose prevail and in them we will never comprehend the vastness of their impact. May God's blessing be upon your family, and their children, and their children, forever.

Looking at your most painful life season through a heavenly lens, how do you see the beautiful power of God?

Heavenly Father, we praise you for your sovereignty and

lordship over every season of our life, and over time itself. God, help us to trust your timing and your purpose through hard times. Cause us to view our circumstances through your heavenly lens so that we may get a glimpse of your glory. May we point others to Jesus through our trials and glorify you always.

In Jesus' holy name. Amen.

"

....
....
....
....
....
....
....
....
....
....
....
....
....
....

Our Contributors

Nancy Kelley Alvarez loves to share stories that inspire risk-taking faith and courage. She believes in making a positive difference in the world one person at a time, through the love of Jesus Christ. She is especially passionate about helping oppressed women and youth survive and thrive in today's challenging world. She leads an online writers' critique group and has authored several devotionals, Bible studies, and Christian fiction. Learn more at https://nancykelleyalvarez.blogspot.com/.

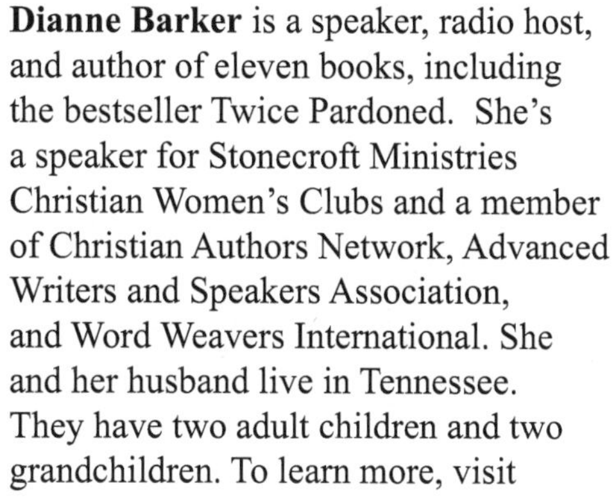

Dianne Barker is a speaker, radio host, and author of eleven books, including the bestseller Twice Pardoned. She's a speaker for Stonecroft Ministries Christian Women's Clubs and a member of Christian Authors Network, Advanced Writers and Speakers Association, and Word Weavers International. She and her husband live in Tennessee. They have two adult children and two grandchildren. To learn more, visit diannebarker.com.

Leigh-Anne Burley was born in Toronto, Ontario, Canada, and resides in Virginia with her husband of 42 years. She has a BA in English and MA in Pastoral Counseling. She is published in nonfiction, fiction, and poetry. Her nonfiction book Beloved by God is available on Amazon and purchased in America and Japan. This book demonstrated with the personal and practical application how intimacy with God is a living reality.

Kasey Burnett is a beloved child of God who is wholeheartedly dedicated to helping people be Heaven-minded. Kasey shares insights for discovering God within the details of life from her own experiences of God's presence, especially during tragedies and losses. Kasey is a wife and mother affectionately serving her family and community in Jefferson, South Carolina.You can connect with Kasey through email at kaseyburnett68@gmail.com.

Pat Butler, author, poet, and pioneer in missional arts, envisions a world in which every Christ follower finds and flourishes in the abundant life Jesus promised. Pat cultivates a global network of artists through writing, mentoring, and spiritual direction. She has traveled to twenty-five countries, lived in two, and holds dual citizenship. Currently residing in Florida, Pat walks with cranes, dodges hurricanes, and enjoys her own pillow.

Penny Cooke is the author of the award-winning book, Pursuing Prayer – Being Effective in a Busy World, in addition to many other compilations, articles and devotions. She is a certified biblical life coach, Bible teacher and speaker whose passion is for believers to be empowered by God's Spirit, His Word, and prayer for this battle we call life. Find her blog, podcast, and more at pennycookeauthor.com.

Jenn Dafoe-Turner is a child of the Highest King. She is a wife of many years to her amazing husband, Ken. Together they have four incredible children, one daughter in love, and three precious grandchildren. Jenn loves to journey with people teaching them to delight in inward truth so they can experience freedom in every area of their lives. She is passionate about the word of God; loves to preach it, teach it and live it. You can connect at www.jenndafoeturner.com

Cherie Denna's mission is to lead others on a sacred discovery toward true belonging in Christ. She is an award-winning author, speaker, and writing coach, passionate about helping people find their voice. Cherie is published in multiple collaborations. You will likely find her at the ocean for seahabilitation, with journal and camera in hand. Cherie resides in Northern California with her husband and looks forward to their next RV adventure. https://cheriedenna.com

Ruth Dyck A third-culture-kid, Ruth Dyck has had many titles over the years, but her favorite are Mom and Grandma. Marrying her Canadian husband, Brian, brought many changes, challenges, joys and adventures over these last thirty-four years. Ruth is working toward a Bachelor's Degree in leadership development at Steinbach Bible College in Manitoba between trips with Brian as missionaries to South Sudan. Find them at appropriatetechnologies.ca.

Todd Ellis You will find the author in the hills of the Midwest writing, hiking and on the farm. His favorite writing includes devotionals and other Christian inspirational messages. He also enjoys authoring how-to manuals that include peak performance and consulting. He also is an avid tennis player and enjoys being on the court.

Nancy Kay Grace offers the hope of grace to those she meets. As a cancer survivor, she understands dealing with unexpected challenges. Because life is unedited—or not perfect—we need God's grace. She is an engaging Bible teacher, speaker, and award-winning author of the devotional The Grace Impact. Nancy is married to her favorite pastor. She loves hugs from grandchildren, playing piano, and hiking. Nancy's blog and GraceNotes newsletter signup are found at nancykaygrace.com.

Ann Griffiths is an author and speaker with a passion to impact future generations. Her calm demeanor and focused drive motivate others to look deep into their own lives, draw out their God-given gifts and abilities, and recognize their profound influence. Ann has extensive leadership experience in business and ministry, lives in British Columbia, Canada with her husband, and loves time with her family and friends.

anngriffiths.com

Mary Harker aims to use the lamp of God's word to shine light into a dark world. She desires to illuminate the path and guide readers in the truth, freedom, hope, and power of Jesus. A contributing author in three WordGirl Collectives and several websites, Mary resides with her people near Rockford, IL. Connect with her at harker.mary96@gmail.com, Facebook @maryjharkerreflects, or Instagram @maryjharker.

Sandra Hastings is a speaker, Bible teacher, and published author. She and her husband spent forty-eight years as Baptist missionaries to the German people. Through this ministry, Sandra interacted with people of many cultural backgrounds, which gave her a strong passion to help believers know and experience their identity in Christ. You can contact Sandra on Facebook, or at AuthorSandraHastings.com

Melissa Heiland is the Founder and President of Beautiful Feet International beautifulfeetinternational.com, a mission organization that has seventy pregnancy centers in twenty-one countries. She is a speaker and author who has written a training manual and curriculum for pregnancy centers, as well as three devotionals. Melissa is the recipient of the 2014 EvanTell Matthew 4:19 award and the 2022 Heartbeat International Servant Leader award.

Sarah Griffiths Hu is a writer and speaker who's passionate about encouraging and equipping women to trust God, surrender their fears, and step into courageous living. She is a self-proclaimed book-buying addict who lives in British Columbia, Canada. Sarah is married and has two adult children and a son-in-love. Connect with Sarah at SarahGriffithsHu.com.

Teresa Janzen, M.Ed., celebrates God's radical abundance as an international author, speaker, coach, and podcast host. More than twenty years of experience in global ministry drives her to share inspiring stories with wit and insight. Married to Dan, together they bridge cultures and continents serving primarily in sub-Saharan Africa and North America. Connect with Teresa at teresajanzen.com and tune-in to Radical Abundance on YouTube or your favorite podcast platform.

Nancy Lee Jenkins is a non-fiction writer, a teacher of bible study groups and a guest speaker. With a passion she created dolls of biblical women, presenting them with their stories in a book titled "Bibledolls". She is currently writing a book about bible women and their connection to today's women. She has worked in church ministry, teaching and preaching for over 46 years. This Devotion was a true experience.

Joylin Lane homeschooled her three children for twelve years and has since returned to teaching elementary age children. She has completed a middle grade book that is ready for publication. She also writes inspirational and nonfiction articles for magazines. She enjoys taking classes at the local college on a variety of topics and is actively involved with three writers groups.

Stacy Leicht has been a teacher for 26 years and currently teaches at UNC-Greensboro. Stacy now resides in North Carolina, where you might find her lounging with a good book in her hand. Stacy continues to instill a love of reading in her students. You can contact Stacy Leicht at leichtse@gmail.com.

Heather MacAskill is a wife, mom to three boys, and an educator. Her journey with Jesus through cancer has inspired her to use every day she has to encourage people. You can share in this journey by connecting with Heather at hmacjourney@gmail.com.

Maureen Miller, wife, mother, and "Mosey," lives on Selah Farm, a hobby homestead nestled in the mountains of western North Carolina. With a passion for God's Word, she writes regularly for several devotion sites, as well as for her local newspaper, and is a contributing author in a variety of collaboratives. Asking to have eyes and ears open to experience God in the miracles of His created world, she blogs weekly at penningpansies.com.

Susanne Moore is an abuse survivor. She empowers women to break free, find healing and embrace Jesus. She is a contributing author in Live and Learn Unexpected Lessons from God's Classroom. She is part of the Well Women Alliance supporting women seeking healing, blog contributor at delightfullyyoursministry.com and loves speaking at women's events. Her home is in Mansfield, Texas. She is currently writing her memoir. You can find her at susanne-moore.com

Chaplain Lisa Northway has been a member of the U.S. Army Chaplaincy for 34 years. She served as a Chaplain Assistant, Chaplain Candidate, and finally a Chaplain since 2005. She has been a Family Life Chaplain since 2016. She is married to Garrett, a Director of Religious Education for the U.S. Army. You can learn more about her ministry at www.lisanorthway.com.

Nancy O'Meara's passion is ministering to women who are transitioning into a new season of life. She loves to introduce Jesus who will give them the tools that they need to embrace change. As a blogger, inspiration speaker, and women's ministry leader, she builds strong relationships helping women adapt finding joy and peace in their journey. Nancy has recently launched "Mid-Week Manna" which can be found at nancyospeaks.com.

Norma Poore, an award winning, Christian writer, is passionate about encouraging others in their faith. She and her husband have been married for forty years. After six children, five in-laws, and eleven grandchildren, she is still crazy about her knight in shining armor. Norma loves to spend time with her loud, crazy family. A foster child herself, Norma and her family fostered children for seven years with more than fifty children gracing their home. Faith, compassion, and fun are behind all Norma does.

Jeanne Roberson is an award-winning author and speaker. Her passion to encourage and inspire others to have faith in God through all circumstances is the driving force behind her message. In her free time, Jeanne enjoys volunteering, gardening, cooking, and spending time with her family. For more information about Jeanne Roberson, visit her at inspiringsouls.com

Betty A Rodgers-Kulich serves with her husband Rick (49 years) as Associate Pastor's at Redeemer's Church, Columbus, Ohio. Director of Women's Ministry for Harvest Preparation International Ministries (Sarasota, Florida) - Mexico and Central America. 2021 CIPA Book Award for General Fiction (The River). Devotional author for Guidepost. Hosting short Facebook videos - ""Life Outside the Pages"", a YouTube channel for Hispanic Women and AWSA P.O.W.E.R. speaker. contact@transformed-image.com"

Chrischa Marie Rosalejos is from Cebu, Philippines. She serves other people all over the globe as a Virtual Assistant through Ripple VA's. She finds honor in knowing, sharing, and witnessing the greatness of God all over the globe from culture to culture. She's in search for the wonders of God life can offer. You can connect with Chrischa through rosalejoschrischamarie@gmail.com

Roberta Sarver taught school, raised a large family, and served as a pastor's wife. Her regular newspaper columns and magazine articles have reflected insight into life's challenging situations. In addition to writing for Abundance Books, Roberta is a contributing author of a children's devotional book, written in International English (publication pending). Her blog Armchair Wit (www.armchairwit.com) garners followers across the nation, yet her greatest accomplishment is being called Mom and living to tell about it.

Leann Seale is a dynamic and engaging speaker, writer, and blogger who is passionate about helping couples build a strong marriage, parenting with purpose and intentionality, and sharing stories of God's faithfulness through the difficult seasons. Leann is a devoted wife, mom to four grown sons, and a daughter of the King. She loves all things sparkly, entertaining people, and traveling. You can read her blog at: LeannSeale.com.

Linda Summerford served on a Foster Care Review Board for two years. Adopted at five with her younger sister, she found out at age 21 that they had an older sister and brother. She determined that she would research what happened to cause their separation. Linda is working diligently for foster care and adoption reforms. Summerford lives in the mountains of Western North Carolina. Connect with Linda at www.authorlindasummerford.com

Lori Vober suffered a hemorrhagic stroke at age twenty-nine, then developed epilepsy from the stroke. She is a walking miracle, and felt called to share her journey of faith and perseverance to encourage others. Even with her difficulties, they were able to become adoptive parents to a sibling group of three. She published her first book, CHOICES: When You Are Faced with a Challenge, What Choice Will You Make? in March 2022. Her website is www.lorivober.com.

Made in the USA
Middletown, DE
11 October 2022

12521252R00102